The Worlds of
DUNE

For my Father, who
gave me *Dune* when
I was far too young

Quarto

First published in 2023 by Frances Lincoln,
an imprint of The Quarto Group.
One Triptych Place, London, SE1 9SH,
United Kingdom
T (0)20 7700 6700
www.Quarto.com

A catalogue record for this book is available
from the British Library.

ISBN 978-0-7112-8211-7
Ebook ISBN 978-0-7112-8212-4

10 9 8 7 6 5 4 3 2 1

Design by Intercity

Printed in China

FRANCES
LINCOLN

The Worlds of

DUNE

*The Places and Cultures
that Inspired Frank Herbert*

TOM HUDDLESTON

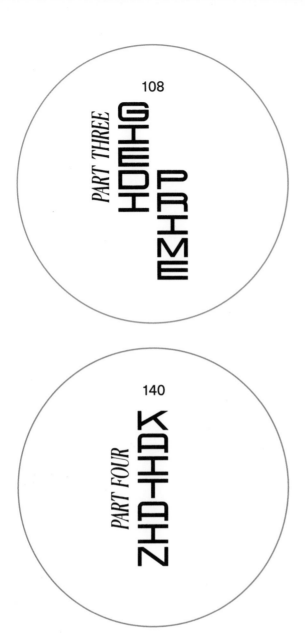

On the publicity trail:
Frank Herbert signing books
in Seattle, 1971

INTRODUCTION

THE
MAKER

Some writers build worlds.
Others birth entire universes.

In the decades since its publication, Frank Herbert's *Dune* has become possibly the best-selling and certainly the best-known science fiction novel ever written, with five sequels by Herbert himself, a vastly expanded multiverse courtesy of elder son Brian and his collaborator Kevin J. Anderson, several major film and TV adaptations, plus numerous role-playing, computer and board games and an ever-growing archive of essays, critical studies and online discussion forums hosting heated debates among fans, scholars and fellow authors. The grand, planet-hopping plot and gallery of indelible and grotesque characters may lure in new readers, but it's the complexity of the novel's themes, the mesmerizing richness of its imagined future and the sheer inventiveness of its construction that keeps them coming back.

So how did an ex-navy newspaperman from Washington State come to write such a world-conquering novel? And how was he able to pack it with so many layers of myth and meaning? From inspiration to publication, *Dune* 'took shape across about six years of research and one-and-a-half years of writing,'[1] according to its author, who read over 200 works of non-fiction[2] and studied everything from Islamic theology to semantic theory, astronomy to Zen Buddhism to Native American tribal ritual. Herbert investigated cutting-edge ideas about ecology and genetics while at the same time drawing on the traditional practices of San tribespeople in Botswana and the lives of the Roman Caesars. He then moulded this research into entirely new and unique shapes, creating a human future that feels at once wholly original and otherworldly, and at the same time ancient, lived-in and thoroughly believable.

In this book we'll explore the diversity of Herbert's influences, from the violent Arabic uprising that prompted the Fremen rebellion on Arrakis to the author's own gaggle of Catholic aunts who would become the Bene Gesserit Sisterhood. We'll look at some of Herbert's literary inspirations, from Edgar Rice Burroughs's swashbuckling Mars sequence to Lawrence of Arabia's self-mythologizing *Seven Pillars of Wisdom*, and we'll also offer a brief study of some of the cultural phenomena that *Dune* would itself inspire, from albums by pop stars, thrash metallers and French synthesiser gurus to the single most successful movie franchise of all time.

But first, let's take a deeper look at the life and formative experiences of the man responsible for all this: writer, reporter, father, photographer, lecturer, speechwriter, sailor, environmental crusader, raconteur, architect, dreamer and all-round renaissance man, Franklin Patrick Herbert Jr.

Quietly radical, deeply knowledgeable and wholly idiosyncratic, Frank Herbert was one of a number of visionary futurists to emerge in America in the decades following the Second World War: we might place him alongside the likes of fellow sci-fi authors Ursula K. Le Guin and Isaac Asimov, *Star Trek* creator Gene Roddenberry and perhaps even Scientology founder and aspirant science-fiction writer L. Ron Hubbard. Largely self-educated and possessed of boundless confidence, each of them would, intentionally or otherwise, inspire cults of feverish enthusiasts eager to examine every detail of their life and work. Herbert may have actively shunned such adulation – his most famous book was, after all, about the perils and pitfalls of hero worship – but that hasn't stopped his devoted fanbase from picking through his writing in search of mystical truths, and claiming *Dune* as a work of almost preternatural prescience.

'Beginnings are such delicate times'

BENE GESSERIT APHORISM, *DUNE*[3]

Frank Herbert was born in the town of Tacoma in Washington State on 8 October 1920, to bus driver Frank Herbert Sr and his wife Eileen, who gave birth on her 19th birthday. Though based in Tacoma, young Frank would spend much of his childhood with his extended family in the nearby town of Burley, on the banks of the saltwater Burley Lagoon. Founded in 1898 as a utopian colony built on socialist principles of collective ownership, Burley was envisioned as a place where 'our children (grow up) close to nature, leading simple, natural lives, and learning that lesson which is so essential for them to know – that the welfare of the individual is inseparably bound up in that of the community.'[4] By the twentieth century, Burley's idealistic past had faded and it had become just 'a busy little bump in the road.'[5] But learning its history would have been Frank's first exposure to alternative ideas of communal living and a society built – at least partly – upon ecological principles.

A voracious and advanced reader from the age of five, Frank would thrill to the cosmic tales of H.G. Wells, Jules Verne and Edgar Rice Burroughs, and later plough happily through the complete works of William Shakespeare and Marcel Proust. But he would also spend a lot of time outdoors: hiking, swimming, boating and camping with his family or by himself, exploring the shores and backwoods of what was, at the time, still a fairly remote corner of the American continent. He would learn the names of plants and animals and the movements of the stars and the tides, becoming a proficient sailor and navigator.

But as he entered his teenage years, Herbert's home life became increasingly fraught. Frank Sr had by this point taken a steady job as a motorbike patrolman for the state police, but he and Eileen were both committed drinkers, and young Frank feared for the safety and well-being of his much younger sister, Patricia. Frank's schoolwork began to suffer, and he was further distracted by his duties as a 'cub reporter' for his high-school newspaper, alongside occasional semi-professional assignments for the local *Tacoma Ledger*. Family struggles came to a head in 1938, forcing Frank to leave home, taking five-year-old Patricia with him, and heading south to the security of his aunt and uncle's home in Salem, Oregon. Patricia would later return to Tacoma, but Frank would stay on in Oregon, where he graduated from high school and by 1940 was working 'on call' at the *Oregon Statesman* newspaper, covering everything from subscriptions and advertising to writing and copy editing.

The following summer, as the Second World War gathered pace, 21-year-old Frank returned to Tacoma to marry Flora Parkinson, a girl he'd only known for a few months. She gave birth to a daughter, Penelope, in February 1942, but by July of that year Frank was gone, having enlisted in the US Navy where he served as a photographer at the Norfolk Naval Shipyard in Portsmouth, Virginia. Following an accident on the base – he tripped over a tent rope and developed a blood clot on his head – Frank was honourably discharged in 1943. But his marriage would not survive: Flora had already requested a divorce and would soon file for custody of their daughter. Frank returned to the Pacific Northwest and to the newspaper trade.

It was here that Frank would meet the love of his life. By the end of the war, he had been through numerous newspaper jobs and sold two short stories to magazines, but he was still eager to widen his horizons. Signing on to study psychology, mathematics and English at the University of Washington, he found himself sharing a

Before the beard: the young
Frank Herbert in Kenwood,
California, c. 1952

creative-writing class with a dark-haired woman of Irish descent named Beverly Stuart Forbes, and was quickly smitten. Following another lightning engagement, they were married in June 1946, and one year later produced their first child, Brian, followed by his brother, Bruce, in 1951.

In the decades that followed, Beverly Herbert would become more to Frank than a wife and partner – she would handle his money and his correspondence, acting as the family's primary breadwinner in times of hardship. She'd support and encourage his writing and his research, remaining his most faithful and enthusiastic reader. And, like many women before and since, she would put her own literary ambitions on permanent hold so that her husband's might flourish.

Throughout the 1950s, the Herbert family moved restlessly, travelling from Seattle, Washington to Santa Rosa, California, where Frank would begin work on his first novel, *Under Pressure*, about the crew of a futuristic submarine dealing with the stresses of war. Then, in 1953, they headed south to Mexico, in the company of Herbert's new friend Jack Vance and his family. Already a respected sci-fi author, Vance would become a key supporter of Herbert's, and vice versa. Their stint in Mexico would only last a few months, but both families would return replete with stories, from run-ins with army generals to Frank's inadvertent first encounter with hallucinogenic substances.

However, Frank's next job would find him stepping into the heart of the political establishment, as he spent several months sans family in Washington, DC, working as a speechwriter for Guy Cordon, Oregon's staunchly conservative Republican senator, who was seeking re-election. The job would hone Herbert's skills as a researcher: Cordon had a particular interest in land use and resource extraction, from logging rights on public land to undersea oil exploration, while also overseeing the committee that supervised America's overseas territories. So, although he was still writing and submitting short stories, Herbert would briefly consider a shift into the political arena, even applying for a government posting to American Samoa, though he was unsuccessful.

When Cordon lost to his Democratic rival, Herbert would return with his family to Tacoma, taking a job with timber lobbying group the Douglas Fir Plywood Association, and finally finding time to complete his first book. *Under Pressure* was serialized in *Astounding Science Fiction* magazine in 1955 and published in a single volume the following year as *The Dragon in the*

Sea, a new title that Herbert suggested at the request of his publisher, though he would continue to favour the original.[6] He would receive the final book proofs while on a second family voyage to Mexico, alongside a rave review in *The New York Times*.

But *The Dragon in the Sea* would prove a critical rather than a popular success, establishing Herbert's sci-fi credentials and allowing him to sell more short stories, but never quite catching the public imagination. A second novel, *Storyship*, would remain unpublished, while another stint in politics, working in public relations for Republican congressional candidate Phil Roth, would result in another lost election. The Herberts were in tricky financial straits, kept afloat by Beverly's job as an advertising copywriter plus occasional proceeds from Frank's writing, such as $4,000 for the film rights to *Under Pressure*. The movie would never be made, but the money came in very useful.

Then, in 1957, a friend from Washington, DC, told Herbert about a research project near Florence, Oregon, where the US Department of Agriculture (USDA) was looking for ways to hold back the encroachment of desert sands on populated areas. Envisioning a magazine article, he began to dig deeper, researching the ecology and history of deserts. The article would never be written, but this tiny spark would ultimately be fanned into a wildfire that would consume Frank Herbert's life.

In a 1969 interview with academic and author Willis E. McNelly, Frank Herbert speaks in detail about his research methods: the reams of file folders he'd amass, the vast quantities of data he'd accumulate, even his reluctance to look something up in the dictionary because he'd just want to keep reading. Once he started investigating the USDA's desert-sands project, things soon began to get out of hand. 'Before long,' he told McNelly, 'I saw that I had far too much for an article, and far too much for a short story . . . I had an enormous amount of data, and avenues shooting off at all angles to gather more, and I was following them.'[7]

Ultimately, Frank Herbert set about answering one intriguing question: 'What if I had an entire planet that was a desert?'[8] He'd already been musing on the idea of writing about a religious leader – to explore, as he put it, 'the messianic convulsions which periodically inflict themselves on human societies'[9] – and these ideas seemed to complement each other perfectly: 'We all know that many religions started in a desert atmosphere, so I decided to put the two together.'[10]

BELOW: The first edition
cover of Herbert's underwater
thriller *The Dragon in the
Sea*, 1956

NEXT PAGE: Paul Atreides
(Timothée Chalamet)
and his mother Jessica
(Rebecca Ferguson) in the
2021 adaptation of *Dune*

'That is the beginning of knowledge – the discovery of something we do not understand'

LETO II,
GOD EMPEROR OF DUNE[11]

From these small origins, an entire galaxy would spring – but it would take time. Herbert would sketch out and then scrap a more traditional sci-fi novel, provisionally entitled *Spice Planet*, following the adventures of an aristocrat named Jesse Linkam who travels from his home planet of Catalan (sic) to the mysterious Duneworld on the orders of the galaxy's Grand Emperor.[12] He would also briefly consider setting his story on Mars, before concluding that the red planet was already too familiar to readers of sci-fi.[13]

The majority of *Dune* would be written in San Francisco, where the family moved in 1960 when Beverly was offered a new job in retail advertising. Frank would take up a position as night-time picture editor with the *San Francisco Examiner*, allowing him the opportunity to write during the day as well as to access the paper's extensive archives. As a fellow journalist recalled: 'Herbert used to come prowling into our book department asking for "anything you have on dry climate ecology" . . . He lusted after the desert, T.E. Lawrence, the Qur'an . . .'[14] Then, in the winter of 1961, he would read to Beverly and Brian a chapter he'd been working on, about a young man forced to undergo a test of pain. It would, he said, be the opening chapter of his new novel.

A brief synopsis of *Dune* is almost impossible, so dense is the book's action and so varied are its ideas. But the essential plot runs as follows: in the year 10,191, during the reign of the Padishah Emperor Shaddam IV, the noble Atreides family journey from the temperate, oceanic world of Caladan to the desert planet of Arrakis, known colloquially as Dune, where they have been tasked with taking control of the production and distribution of melange, a naturally occurring spice so powerful that it extends human life and gives the user the gift of limited prescience. But the Atreides have been lured into a trap set by their ancestral enemies the Harkonnens, who launch a surprise attack, leading to the death of Duke Leto Atreides and driving his concubine Jessica and their son Paul out into the unforgiving deserts of Arrakis.

Here they make contact with the Fremen, a tribal society of desert dwellers who have been working in secret to transform Arrakis from a wasteland into a paradise. Allying himself with their cause, Paul takes on the Fremen name of Muad'dib and sparks a revolutionary war against the Harkonnens and the Emperor. In the process he becomes a messiah to the Fremen, using the spice to attain powers of extraordinary foresight. In the final battle for control of Arrakis, Paul defeats his enemies and takes the imperial throne for himself, opening the floodgates for his Fremen followers to launch a galactic jihad – a holy war.

The novel ultimately published as *Dune* was initially serialized in *Analog* magazine in two parts, across eight issues: 'Dune World' ran from December 1963 to February 1964,[15] with 'The Prophet of Dune' following from January to May of 1965.[16] Herbert had accepted the advice of *Analog*'s editor John W. Campbell, author of the sci-fi classic 'Who Goes There?'[17] (filmed as *The Thing*), to help him hone and clarify his ideas, though the two didn't always see eye to eye: Campbell found Muad'dib's gift of prescience problematic, but Herbert fought his corner.[18]

The single-volume edition of *Dune* was published in 1965, though only after 'more than 12 publishers had turned it down,'[19] according to its disgruntled author. It would eventually find a home with Chilton Books, whose main area of business was publishing auto-repair manuals, and who released the book with little fanfare. Under these circumstances, it's unsurprising that *Dune* was not an immediate best seller. But science-fiction fans and fellow authors recognized its brilliance right away: in 1966 it won the inaugural Nebula Award – now

considered one of the top prizes in science fiction – and shared the Hugo Award for Best Novel with Roger Zelazny's *This Immortal*.[20] Many reviews were gushing, with prominent figures including Arthur C. Clarke lining up to sing the book's praises (one notable outlier was J.R.R. Tolkien, who claimed to 'dislike *Dune* with some intensity'[21] – although, to be fair, it's hard to imagine two more opposing authorial temperaments than placid Oxford don Tolkien and brash autodidact Herbert).

In the coming decade, *Dune*'s reputation would grow steadily. After all, its themes could have been tailor-made for the 1960s, covering, as *Dune* scholar Daniel Immerwahr writes: 'environmentalism, psychedelic drugs, mysticism, orgies, back-to-the-land survivalism, indigenous ways, anticolonial rebellions, Arab nationalism, and political assassinations.'[22] Alongside *The Lord of the Rings* it would become a staple on university campuses: Herbert may not have had much time for the hippies, according to Brian, but they nonetheless took to him.

The book's first sequel, *Dune Messiah*, would arrive in 1969 and spark immediate controversy. Much shorter than its predecessor, *Messiah* found Herbert determined to overturn much of what came before, exposing the wild cruelty of Muad'dib's galactic jihad and painting Paul as a helpless figure trapped by his messianic status and his 'gift' of prescience, which has left his life empty of surprises. Concerned more with conspiracy and personal tragedy than sweeping action, the book would prove that, unlike Paul, Herbert would refuse to be bound by the expectations of his followers.

But *Dune* wasn't Herbert's only focus. Throughout this period he was prodigiously productive, publishing three short story collections and 10 novels between the concluding part of *Dune* in 1965 and a second sequel, *Children of Dune*, in 1976. Among these would be several of his best-known non-*Dune* works, including anti-utopian fable *The Santaroga Barrier* (1968), religious science-fiction epic *The Godmakers* (1972) and insect-inspired conspiracy thriller *Hellstrom's Hive* (1973). The film rights to *Dune* would be first picked up in 1971, and three years later pre-production began on the first attempt to film the book, headed by Chilean mystic Alejandro Jodorowsky. That film would, famously, never be completed, but we'll explore *Dune*'s journey to the screen in more detail in the epilogue to this volume.

In 1972, with both of their sons now flown the nest, Frank and Beverly Herbert used the growing proceeds from sales of *Dune* and its sequel to purchase a farm and

'A man is a fool not to put everything he has, at any given moment, into what he is creating'

FRANK HERBERT[23]

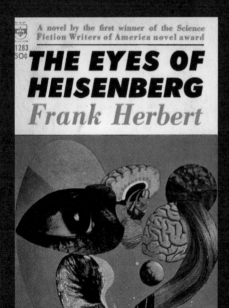

2.4 hectares (6 acres) near Port Townsend, Washington, in the same region where Frank had grown up. Naming it Xanadu after the fabled palace of Kublai Khan, Frank set about turning the farm into what he called his Ecological Demonstration Project – a forward-thinking exercise in sustainable living complete with windmills, orchards and vineyards; ducks, geese and chickens; hybrid rice plants and greenhouses filled with citrus trees. The project would be derailed, however, when in 1974 Beverly was diagnosed with lung cancer, an illness which would lead to repeated bouts of hospitalization over the coming years.

Children of Dune would be Herbert's first out-of-the-gate best seller – in fact, the first hardback science-fiction best seller ever. Focusing on Paul's twin children Leto II and Ghanima, the book further unpicks the myth of Muad'dib, as these preternaturally aware 10-year-olds search for a way to halt the destructive galactic crusade and undo the damage wrought by their father's messianic rise. The last in the series to feature beloved characters

like Lady Jessica, weapons master Gurney Halleck and even an appearance from the deceased Baron Harkonnen, the book marks the conclusion of the original trilogy – but not of the *Dune* series.

In 1980, with Beverly still suffering from ill health, the Herberts would purchase a large plot of shoreline property on the Hawaiian island of Maui, where they planned to build a new home to Frank's own design. The idea was that Beverly's lungs would benefit from a warmer climate, but Frank's increasing work demands and the slow pace of progress on the building made life as busy as ever. The following year would see the publication of *God Emperor of Dune,* the fourth and strangest of the series, focusing again on Paul's son Leto Atreides II, who after 3,500 years of steady mutation has transformed himself into a monstrous, dictatorial sandworm hybrid, ruling a static empire from the now verdant world of Arrakis. Consisting to a large extent of heady philosophical, political and sociological discussions between Leto and his cadre of underlings

LEFT: In Xanadu: The author in his home office at Port Townsend, 1979

ABOVE AND RIGHT: Action! Frank Herbert holds the clapperboard for director David Lynch (top) on the first day of shooting his 1984 adaptation of *Dune*, starring Kyle MacLachlan (bottom) as Paul Atreides

– whose ranks include the revived 'ghola' of his father's long-dead sword master Duncan Idaho – the book was nonetheless a huge seller.

But, despite the move to Hawaii and a number of successful surgeries, Beverly's health stubbornly refused to improve. In 1984 a big-budget *Dune* movie, directed by highly regarded newcomer David Lynch and featuring an extraordinary cast of notable thespians, would finally be released into cinemas. The same year would see the publication of the fifth novel in the series, *Heretics of Dune*, alongside a somewhat sillier addition to the *Dune*iverse: *National Lampoon's Doon*,[24] a novel-length parody following the adventures of Paul Mauve'bib on the dessert planet Arruckus, as an intergalactic war breaks out for control of the mysterious intoxicating substance known as beer.

But all of this would be overshadowed by Beverly's death in February – 'a peaceful passing . . . without fear or tears,'[25] as Frank wrote on the morning after her death. With Beverly gone, Frank lost his greatest champion, the woman who kept his personal life on track, allowing him to focus on work to the exclusion of all else. Very soon, his own health would begin to suffer.

Heretics of Dune was intended to mark the beginning of a new phase for the *Dune* series, moving the action forward another 1,500 years and centring now on the Bene Gesserit Sisterhood, an ancient order of female mystics whose efforts to maintain galactic stability are undermined by the Honoured Matres, a cabal of monstrous warrior women who use sex as a weapon of control. But following the cliffhanger conclusion of the next volume, *Chapterhouse: Dune*, in 1985, the series would remain unfinished. *Chapterhouse* would, however, conclude with a heartfelt tribute to Beverly: 'Is it any wonder,' Frank wrote, 'that I look back on our years together with a happiness transcending anything words can describe?'[26] For a writer of his talents, that's quite an admission.

Frank Herbert's remaining years would be typically busy, working on a collaborative novel with his son Brian and entering into a short-lived third marriage to a publisher's representative named Teresa Shackleford. He made notes for a seventh *Dune* novel, but these would prove too sketchy for publication – instead, Brian Herbert and his collaborator Kevin J. Anderson would wrap up the *Dune* saga with a pair of novels tying up the threads left by *Chapterhouse: Dune* – *Hunters of Dune* and *Sandworms of Dune* – while also providing readers with an ongoing series of prequel and 'interquel' novels that slot between the novels of the official Frank Herbert canon. However, while this volume will respect Brian Herbert and Kevin J. Anderson's work, their books will not be covered in any detail.

On 11 February 1986, almost exactly two years after Beverly's passing, Frank Herbert succumbed to a pulmonary embolism while recovering from surgery for pancreatic cancer. By that point *Dune* had become a best seller many times over, and its impact could be felt across the cultural spectrum, from the desert landscapes and mystical forces of the *Star Wars* saga to the increasing significance of the ecological movement. It has become a staple on lists of the most important novels ever written, has been vital to the acceptance of science fiction as a valid literary form, and with the release of director Denis Villeneuve's two-part film adaptation its influence has spread even further.

But what remains most remarkable about *Dune* is how complex, how rich, how abundant the book is. In his research, Frank Herbert tugged on so many disparate threads that the result could have been a confusion of tangled ideas, a conceptual labyrinth with no way out. Instead, thanks to the author's unerring sense of narrative and his deft feeling for character, *Dune* is an entirely cohesive and consistently entertaining read; a book that can be experienced simply as a gripping intergalactic yarn or, for those willing to dig a little deeper, as a complex interweaving of scientific inquiry, historical study, political theory and religious philosophy.

For those in the latter camp, we now present a planet-by-planet guide to the worlds of *Dune*, hoping to enrich and enliven the reader's experience of particularly the first novel, but also its five sequels. This book is intended to stand as a tribute to Frank Herbert's life and work, to the breadth and detail of his research, and to the sheer imaginative brilliance of his writing.

Marital bliss: Beverly and Frank Herbert relaxing at home, Port Townsend, 1979

'A man's flesh is his own; the water belongs to the tribe'

FREMEN SAYING, *DUNE* [27]

PART ONE

ARRAKIS

CHAPTER ONE

DESERT PLANET

The science of ecology – simply put, the study of the relationships between living things and their environment – is at the very core of *Dune*. The book is dedicated to 'the dry-land ecologists, wherever they may be,'[1] and was principally intended as 'an ecological novel . . . with many overtones, as well as a story about people and their human concerns'.[2] This preoccupation with the environment is embodied most clearly in the world at the centre of the book: 'Arrakis, the planet known as Dune.'[3]

Alongside the written word, the wilderness was Frank Herbert's first love. And although the parched deserts of Arrakis may bear little similarity to the oyster-rich lagoons, forested peninsulas and teeming trout streams of his Pacific childhood, still Frank grew up among wild places, developing an enthusiasm for exploration that would last a lifetime. Indeed, following his marriage to Beverly in 1946, the couple would spend a four-month honeymoon occupying a remote cabin atop Kelly Butte, a 1.6-kilometre (5,400-foot) peak in the Cascade Mountains of Washington State, where Frank had been employed as a fire-watcher ('The biggest fire in the woods was us,' Beverly would wryly claim).[4]

But in the late 1950s and early 1960s, when Frank Herbert was researching and writing *Dune*, he wasn't the only one captivated by America's natural bounty. The US conservation movement had been around since before Frank's birth, when the popular success of Henry David Thoreau's nature-exalting 1854 memoir *Walden*[5] sparked a popular campaign to protect the wilderness from voracious logging and mining interests. Spearheaded by President-to-be Theodore Roosevelt and his pioneering Boone and Crockett Club, the movement would lobby for the expansion of the National Parks programme, leading to the establishment in 1905 of the United States Forest Service.

Two World Wars and one Great Depression may have diverted political priorities in the USA, but by the 1950s the preservation of wilderness was back on the agenda. With the rise in disposable income came a renewed eagerness to engage with the Great Outdoors: while in 1943 the United States Forest Service estimated that some 1.1 million overnight campers had made use of its services, by 1960 that number had risen to 10.9 million.[6] Similarly, though only 19 people would take the Colorado River route through the Grand Canyon in 1952, just 20 years later that number was over 16,000.[7]

At the same time, the burgeoning back-to-the-land movement would result in the publication of several *Walden*-like memoirs of a retreat from urban spaces, from Betty MacDonald's *The Egg and I*[8] to Helen and Scott Nearing's *Living the Good Life*[9] – not to mention Beat-icon Jack Kerouac's *The Dharma Bums*, which in part recounts his 63 days spent as a fire-watcher on Desolation Peak, not too many miles from the Herberts' own Kelly Butte.[10] In the ensuing decade, countless American citizens would make the move from city to country, from the largely ill-fated communes that sprung up in the hippie era to cultists and survivalists looking to exercise their constitutional freedoms away from prying eyes.

In 1964, the Wilderness Act would be signed into American law, codifying the preservation of wild spaces 'for the permanent good of the whole people'. The Act would define the meaning of wilderness in no uncertain terms, as 'an area where the earth and its community of life are untrammelled by man, where man himself is a visitor who does not remain'.[11]

But it would be a single, obscure ecological project that would plant the seeds of *Dune*. In 1957, a political acquaintance encouraged Frank Herbert to pay a visit to a US Department of Agriculture (USDA) research station near Florence, Oregon, which was pioneering a successful experiment in controlling what was called 'desert creep'. Throughout human history deserts have been on the move – indeed, large parts of the Sahara were once fertile and populated, before the sand consumed them. In Oregon, the dunes had advanced on the town of Florence, swallowing farms, buildings, railroads and highways. But after years of experimentation, the USDA had found a solution: by planting so-called 'poverty grasses' – plants that thrive in poor or sandy soil, widely

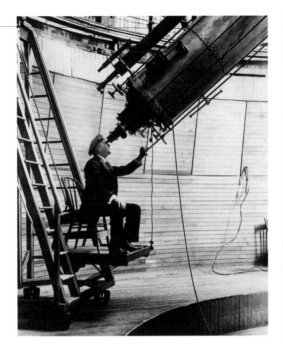

LEFT: Astronomer Percival
Lowell at the scientific
institute which bears his
name: the Lowell Observatory
in Flagstaff, Arizona

RIGHT: A 1927 edition of
Amazing Stories magazine
featuring a serialization
of H.G. Wells's The War
of the Worlds

BOTTOM: The Oregon Dunes
National Recreation Area
near Florence was one of the
initial inspirations for Dune

grown as fodder during the Depression – they had been able to stabilize and even turn back the dunes. Already, scientists and policymakers from several interested nations, including Egypt, Chile and Israel, were coming to study the project and learn from it.[12]

His interest piqued, Herbert chartered a Cessna prop plane and flew to Florence to take photographs and make notes for a proposed magazine article that he intended to name 'They Stopped the Moving Sands'. Foreseeing an ecological study coupled with an attention-grabbing human-interest angle, Herbert was disappointed when his literary agent – a bullish New Yorker with the grandiose name of Lurton Blassingame – exhibited little interest ('it is fairly limited in appeal', he wrote).[13]

The article would ultimately be shelved, but the idea stuck with Herbert and refused to shift. What, he wondered, would happen if the deserts were allowed to creep indefinitely? Would they eventually swallow the entire planet? And if so, could a project like the one pioneered by the USDA work on a global scale – could a planet that had been lost to desert one day become habitable again? In pondering such ecological questions on a global rather than a local scale, Frank Herbert was some way ahead of his time: the best-known work on this subject, chemist James Lovelock's 'whole earth' Gaia hypothesis, wouldn't be published until 1972.[14]

But Herbert wasn't the first to posit the idea of a planetary desert. Towards the end of the nineteenth century, American businessman, astronomer and telescope-builder Percival Lowell had begun speculating that the lines which he and others had apparently observed on the surface of Mars were in fact canals, constructed by some ancient but advanced Martian culture. He even believed he could make out a number of 'oases' – dark spots where two or more of these canals converged.[15] Across three scientific studies Lowell expanded his theory, suggesting that these canals had been built by a now-dead civilization to channel water from the planetary poles, in an effort to survive on a planet that was rapidly drying out and turning to desert.

Lowell's ideas have, of course, been conclusively disproved – the canals are now believed to have been some kind of optical illusion. But the idea of a planetary civilization dying from a lack of water was a powerful one. Among those who took inspiration were author H.G. Wells, whose Martian invaders in The War of the Worlds hail from just such a world: he writes that they 'regarded this Earth with envious eyes, and slowly and surely drew their plans against us'.[16] Some years later, Tarzan creator Edgar Rice Burroughs would begin serializing his Barsoom stories set on an ecologically damaged Mars, while authors Robert Heinlein and Ray Bradbury would both feature the Martian canals in their novels.

Of course, the idea of a planet drying up and turning to dust wasn't an entirely fanciful one, particularly for Americans in the mid-twentieth century. A more earthbound influence on the ecology of Arrakis must have been the Great Depression that Herbert lived through, and the horrifying dust storms and famines that accompanied it. The author was particularly informed by the work of Paul Bigelow Sears, an American scientist whose 1935 book Deserts on the March[17] attempted to offer ecological solutions to an American readership suffering the ravages of the Dust Bowl. By pinpointing the way humans were affecting their environment through deforestation and soil erosion, leading inevitably to the 'desertification' witnessed during the Depression, Sears brought home the direct impact of ecology on everyday American life and provided suggestions to prevent it from happening again.

Later named President of the Ecological Society of America, the American Association of Science and the American Society of Naturalists, Sears's work would inform the budding green movement and prove vital to Dune. Indeed, one of the ecologist's

LEFT: The ravages of the
American Dust Bowl of the
1930s, as farms in Guymon,
Oklahoma (top) and South
Dakota (bottom) are
swallowed up

RIGHT: Conservationist
Rachel Carson, author of the
influential *Silent Spring*

own aphorisms – 'the highest function of science is to give us an understanding of consequences' – would be repeated almost word-for-word in Herbert's book, placed in the mouth of another ecologist, Pardot Kynes;[18] while another – 'respect for truth comes close to being the basis for all morality' – would be taught to Paul Atreides by his father.[19]

Sears was among the first thinkers to place humanity within – rather than somehow outside or above – their environment, exploring how our actions affect the world around us, and how those effects then rebound on humanity. This concept of ecology as an interlinked system is vital to *Dune*, where everything that occurs has effects that ripple outward through the book and its sequels. As Pardot Kynes says in *Dune*'s appendices: 'The thing the ecologically illiterate don't realize about an ecosystem is that it's a system . . . A system has order, flowing from point to point. If something dams that flow, order collapses.'[20]

Another book that would inform the ecological message of the *Dune* series – and indeed the environmental movement as a whole – was *Silent Spring*,[21] published in 1962 by marine biologist and conservationist Rachel Carson and widely read throughout the coming decade. Convinced that several apparently unconnected environmental problems – among them the unexplained death of bird life and aquatic fauna, and a rise in cancers among the human population – could be traced to a single source, namely the widespread spraying of pesticides like DDT, Carson decided to lay out her arguments in a work of popular ecology rather than a scientific paper. Much to the annoyance of the chemical companies, the book was a huge success, spurring the creation of the Environmental Protection Agency under the Nixon administration in 1970 and a countrywide ban on DDT usage two years later.[22]

For Herbert, the key aspect of Carson's book was how she laid out in plain terms the negative effects of human tampering with the natural world as well as the invisible links between seemingly isolated environmental problems, for example the way that a chemical intended to kill pests could get into the food chain and affect other forms of life, including humans. Both Carson's and Sears's work has been labelled 'apocalyptic ecology,'[23] in that each warned of potentially devastating global consequences if certain key ecological red flags were ignored – consequences that we, in the twenty-first century, are all too familiar with.

Herbert's vision of Arrakis may be the ultimate in apocalyptic ecology: here is a world utterly altered by ecological change, bringing it to the verge of human uninhabitability. But the book also offers the possibility of transformation. Decades before the events depicted in *Dune*, imperial ecologist Pardot Kynes devised a plan to capture every drop of moisture on the planet and use it to seed Arrakis with water-retaining plants and – of course – poverty grasses. This ecological revolution is not expected to be swift: indeed, Kynes sets out an initial timeline of three to five centuries. But he has a secret weapon: an entire population bent on the task of terraforming Dune. 'What a tool they could be!' Kynes realizes. 'Fremen: an ecological and geological force of almost unlimited potential.'[24]

This is one of the reasons *Dune* was adopted by the environmental movement: for its vision of an entire planetary community working towards a single environmental goal, and of ecological necessity assuming a central role in every human life. This may seem utopian, but it could offer a way out of the environmental disaster in which humanity currently finds itself. And the patience of the Fremen is inexhaustible: 'Our generation will not see it,' the tribal leader Stilgar tells Jessica, 'nor our children nor our children's children nor the grandchildren of their children ... but it will come.'[25]

Saving the planet: volunteers work to remove invasive buffelgrass from Saguaro National Park East, Arizona

✳

In a letter to Lurton Blassingame regarding 'They Stopped the Moving Sands', Frank Herbert likens desert dunes to ocean waves, 'except that they move 20 feet a year instead of 20 feet a second. These waves can be every bit as devastating as a tidal wave'.[26] This equivalence between the desert and the ocean clearly fascinated Herbert – in his interview with Willis McNelly he speaks of 'fluid mechanics with sand', and how those who come to view sand dunes as akin to water can 'learn to control them'.[27]

The image of the desert as an ocean recurs throughout *Dune*, with rock formations described as 'lifting like islands',[28] or the desert as 'a static ocean ... full of moon-silvered waves'.[29] The Fremen themselves often resemble bands of sailors, equipped with charts, maps and arcane knowledge, navigating by compass and the stars from one safe harbour to another.

A lifelong sailor himself, Herbert had grown up beside the ocean and as a young reader had devoured seagoing adventure stories like Jules Verne's *20,000 Leagues Under the Sea* – indeed, his own first novel, *Under Pressure*, was also set in the belly of a submarine. He would purchase two sailboats with the proceeds from *Dune*, christening the first *Caladan* after the Atreides' ocean-rich home world and the second *Ghanima* after the young heroine of *Children of Dune,* herself named for a Fremen (and Arabic) word meaning 'spoils of war'.

But there is another parallel between *Dune* and oceanic yarns like *20,000 Leagues Under the Sea* and Herman Melville's *Moby-Dick*. In Verne's book, the advanced submarine *Nautilus* is attacked by a school of giant squid while on manoeuvres in the Atlantic, while *Moby-Dick* is of course about the hunt for a legendary white whale, huge in size and seemingly ageless. There's a leviathan in *Dune*, too, lurking beneath the dusty oceans of Arrakis: the giant sandworm, known to the Fremen as *shai hulud*, 'the maker', and viewed by them as a god.

For Frank Herbert, 'the origins of the sandworm were right out of Sir James Frazer's *The Golden Bough*[30].'[31] In this seminal study of myth and religion, Scottish anthropologist Frazer examined legends and religious texts from across the globe to find points of comparison, among them recurring images of dragons and sea monsters that appear in everything from the Greek myths to the Biblical books of Job and Jonah. The traditional significance of the serpent – who rises from the deep to devour young virgins – is somewhat obvious, but for Herbert the sandworm represented something different: something more aligned to the work of his contemporary, J.R.R. Tolkien.

To create *shai hulud*, Herbert took inspiration from the dragons and serpents – often referred to as 'wyrms' – that appear throughout European mythology, notably in the old English story of the warrior king, Beowulf. While the earlier parts of this legend, featuring the monster Grendel and his equally hideous mother, may be better known to modern audiences, in the final part of the legend Beowulf confronts a dragon who has ravaged his lands as revenge for the theft of a cup, much like Smaug in Tolkien's *The Hobbit*. Beowulf battles the beast and kills it, but dies in the attempt.

Herbert himself would describe the sandworm as 'the archetypal black beast, the one who lives underground in the cavern, with the gold',[32] or 'the mindless guardians of the terrible treasure . . . the dragon who carries the pearl of great price in its mouth.'[33] In this analogy, the gold or 'pearl of great price' is the spice melange, whose link to the worm is revealed to Paul when he becomes stranded in the desert. The life cycle of the worm will become vital to the *Dune* series, as Herbert explores the creature's development from the larval worm (or 'sandtrout'), to the juvenile worm that is ritually drowned by the Fremen to create the Water of Life, to the full-grown worm of whom the spice is a mysterious by-product. But in its initial appearances – for the characters as much as for the reader – the worm is something more instinctively terrifying, the dark terror from the depths that lurks in our most ancient nightmares.

But the sandworm isn't the greatest danger to human life on Arrakis. The desert itself is an even more deadly foe, and *Dune* is as much a tale of survival as it is a science-fiction story. The attention Herbert pays to the Fremen practices of 'moisture security' and 'desert discipline' is painstaking, from the rigorous necessity of sealing every room to the 'stilltent, energy caps, recaths, sandsnork, binoculars, stillsuit repkit, baradye pistol, sinkchart, filt-lugs, paracompass, maker hooks, thumpers . . .'[34] that Paul finds in his 'fremkit' – the ultimate desert survival pack.

Many of these tools derive entirely from Frank Herbert's imagination, but he also took inspiration from the real world, notably the survival practices employed by the San people of the Kalahari Desert in Botswana. Like Arrakis, the Kalahari has transformed over millennia from a fertile, water-rich region to a parched wasteland, as tectonic movement lifted the plateau, shifted the paths of rivers and drained entire lakes, turning them to mudflats and finally to desert.[35] In the process, plant, animal and human life was forced to adapt or be destroyed – among them the San, one of the most ancient cultures on the planet.

TOP LEFT: Captain Nemo vs the giant squid: a 19th-century illustration from *20,000 Leagues Under the Sea*

TOP RIGHT: The great wyrm: Beowulf faces the dragon in this 1916 illustration

BOTTOM: An 1892 illustration depicting the Masarwa hunters of the North Kalahari Desert

NEXT PAGE: Gods, what a monster! The Giant Sandworm of Arrakis as seen in the 2021 film

TOP: Jessica, Chani, Stilgar and Paul demonstrate the correct use of a stillsuit in 2021's *Dune*

BOTTOM: Influential anthropologist Sir Laurens van der Post

"It was sea and air power on Caladan," he said. "Here, it's desert power."

PAUL ATREIDES, *DUNE* [36]

Nomadic hunter-gatherers who congregate in bands and family groups, the San are unique in their ability to exist in some of the most unforgiving environments on earth, where their day-to-day survival requires extraordinary discipline. To conserve energy, the San often spend their daylight hours almost entirely motionless, inching through patches of shade and breathing through the nose to limit the loss of moisture – a lesson also espoused by the Fremen. They sit on mats or blankets to avoid direct contact with the heated ground, and in extreme circumstances might completely bury themselves in sand, even soaking it with urine to cool it further.[37] They are familiar with every plant that hoards moisture, from edible succulents and tubers to wild desert cucumbers, and were the original consumers of a medicinal plant named Hoodia, which has now been scientifically recognized as a natural appetite suppressant.[38]

Herbert may have been familiar with the San via the work of controversial South African author and anthropologist Laurens van der Post, whose 1956 BBC documentary series *The Lost World of the Kalahari* and its best-selling 1958 tie-in book[39] first brought the San and their culture to global attention. A widely travelled soldier with the British Army during the Second World War, van der Post's work as an anthropologist would make him a household name in the UK: in later years he would become close friends with Prince (now King) Charles, and godfather to his son and heir, William. Referring to the San as 'the bushmen of the Kalahari' – a name that stuck for decades but which is now viewed as pejorative – van der Post may have elevated their culture in the eyes of the world, but his view of the San as mystical 'lost souls' has since been seen as somewhat patronizing and Euro-centric.[40]

But perhaps the most notable item of desert survival gear found in *Dune* was one dreamed up entirely by Herbert. The stillsuit is a garment that allows its wearer to survive for days, even in the deep desert, by conserving almost every drop of the body's moisture. Described by the ecologist Liet-Kynes as 'a high-efficiency filter and heat-exchange system'[41] wherein sweat, breath and even urine and faeces are recaptured and purified, the stillsuit is manufactured by the Fremen to exacting specifications. And while Frank Herbert would have been familiar with existing 'closed loop' survival systems such as spacesuits, orbital capsules and diving bells, no one had ever imagined a desert suit that could recycle the body's own water.

But the stillsuit is more than just a practicality. It is the daily garb and emblem of the inhabitants of Arrakis: that mysterious race of people who for decades have guarded a great secret from their oppressors the Harkonnens, from the agents of the Spacing Guild, and even from the eyes of the Emperor.

CHAPTER TWO
THE FREMEN

Rebel warlord and religious
revolutionary: Imam Shamil,
the Lion of Dagestan

In the mid-nineteenth century, under the banner
of Imam Shamil (or Shamyl), the Lion of Dagestan,
an unprecedented truce was brokered between the
Islamic tribes of the Northern Caucasus Mountains.
After centuries of in-fighting, these hard-living
nomadic peoples banded together to wage holy
war against the Russian imperialists who had invaded
their lands, conducting a fierce guerrilla campaign
that would last more than a quarter of a century.
The campaign may have ended in defeat – indeed,
the area remains under Russian control to this day,
separated into regions such as Ingushetia, Chechnya,
Dagestan and others. But Shamil's revolutionary
campaign would leave an unexpected literary legacy.

Imam Shamil was a figure of legend, even among his own people. Simultaneously a political, military and religious leader – his official title was Third Imam of the Caucasian Imamate – he was known as a man of great personal charisma and unflinching piety, treating all his tribal followers equally according to the dictates of his faith.[1] His campaign would suffer numerous setbacks: in 1839, Shamil and 4,000 of his followers, including women and children, were besieged in the rock fortress of Akhulgo, deep in the mountains. The ensuing 80-day blockade would claim hundreds of lives on both sides, including those of Shamil's second wife and his sister, before Shamil's forces withdrew. But his triumphs were every bit as extraordinary. In 1843 his forces swept through the region of Avaria, capturing every Russian outpost but one and inflicting over 2,000 casualties. The Russians rallied, sending a 10,000 strong army against Shamil. But it wasn't enough, as Shamil's forces pursued the Russians into the forests of Chechnya, where they surrounded and destroyed them.[2]

The rebellion was doomed to failure – in 1856 the Russians sent 250,000 men to the Caucasus, and while tribal resistance was fierce and sustained, the invaders were simply better trained, better armed and far more numerous. In 1859, Imam Shamil was shipped in chains to St Petersburg, where he met with Tsar Nicholas II. Perhaps surprisingly, he was allowed to live out the rest of his life in relative luxury, occupying a comfortable house in Kiev from where he corresponded regularly with his sons, and in 1869 even performed the Hajj, the pilgrimage to Mecca.

Of course, the conflict between the Russian state and the Islamic peoples of Chechnya and the wider Caucasus would not end with Shamil – over 150 years later, that war goes on. But the legend of the Lion of Dagestan would continue to grow, sparking imaginations across the world. In 1960, British historian, travel writer and socialite Lesley Blanch would publish a definitive narrative history of the Imam's life and military exploits entitled *The Sabres of Paradise*: a gripping, richly researched romance that would prove a vital wellspring for Frank Herbert's *Dune*.[3]

Blanch herself was a remarkable figure, her career ranging from a wartime stint as the features editor at UK *Vogue* to the publication of several books of non-fiction including *The Wilder Shores of Love*,[4] a look at the lives of four women who left Europe for the Middle East, and *Farah, Shahbanou of Iran*,[5] a biography of her acquaintance Farah Pahlavi, the exiled widow of the last Iranian Shah. Blanch would travel the world as the wife of French diplomat, novelist and filmmaker Romain Gary (who would in turn leave her for the actress Jean Seberg). In 2001 she was awarded an MBE by the British government, followed by the French *Officier de l'Ordre des Arts et des Lettres* in 2004, three years before her death at the age of 102.

Blanch's influence on Herbert's writing is incalculable. Several direct quotes from *The Sabres of Paradise* can be found in *Dune*, from the plea opposite, found scrawled on the outer wall of the Arrakeen spaceport,[6] to two key lessons learned by Paul Atreides: 'to kill with the point (or tip) lacks artistry', and the Caucasian proverb 'polish comes from the city, wisdom from the hills' (or, in *Dune*, the desert).[7]

Many Caucasian words also made the transition from Blanch's book: *chakobsa*, one of the ancient hunting languages of the Caucasus, is also a secret tongue known to the Fremen and the Bene Gesserit; *Padishah*, the imamate's name for the Russian Tsar, is the hereditary title of the Emperor in *Dune*; while the *kindjal*, a double-edged blade worn by the warriors who followed Shamil, was rediscovered several millennia later by the nobles of Herbert's universe. And Herbert didn't just acquire terms from Blanch's Islamic revolutionaries: the name Sietch Tabr, Muad'dib's hidden home on

LEFT: Imam Shamil surrenders to the Russian General Count Baryatinsky, from an 1880 painting by Alexei Danilovich Kivshenko

RIGHT: Lesley Blanch visits Wadi Rum in Jordan, 1965

'O! You who know what we suffer here, do not forget us in your prayers!'

CAUCASIAN CAPTIVES
QUOTED IN *THE SABRES OF PARADISE*[8]

Part One: Arrakis

'It's well known that repression makes a religion flourish'

THUFIR HAWAT, DUNE [9]

Arrakis, combines two words for 'camp' from the language of the Cossacks: Tsarist warriors who were the sworn enemies of Shamil's people.

But the influence of *The Sabres of Paradise* isn't just detectable in the language. As writer Will Collins observes in his essay 'The Secret History of *Dune*', Blanch's vivid account of a fierce, religiously motivated guerilla war between the oppressed population of a remote, inhospitable region and a far mightier, technologically advanced imperial force is the very bedrock of Herbert's novel,[10] while her vivid depiction of Shamil must surely have made an impression on the author. In one memorable passage, she quotes a Russian soldier at the Battle of Gimry in 1832 – during which Shamil killed three men only to be bayoneted by a fourth – who recalls that: 'He seized the bayonet, pulled it out of his own flesh, cut down the man, and with another superhuman leap, cleared the wall and vanished in the darkness.'[11] As with Muad'dib, the dividing line between man and myth has grown faint indeed.

A thrilling depiction of the Battle of Gimry by Franz Roubaud, 1891

The Fremen are the wild heart of *Dune*. Grim, ruthless and unsentimental, these desert-dwelling tribes are also fiercely loyal, deeply spiritual, near-matchless in battle and entirely justified in their struggle for freedom. But while the Fremen may have survived on Arrakis for many centuries – a harsh existence that has honed them into fierce warriors – they are not native to this world. Indeed, Herbert explicitly writes that the Fremen are the descendants of an ancient Islamic diaspora: 'We are the people of *Misr*,' Reverend Mother Ramallo laments, invoking an Arabic word for Egypt.[12] 'Since our Sunni ancestors fled from *Nilotic al-Ourouba* (or Nile valley) we have known flight and death.'[13] These very specific origins are directly reflected in the Fremen language, culture, traditions and religious practices.

This unbroken link between the Fremen and their Arabic ancestors has made some readers of *Dune* uncomfortable, given that the novel is the work of a white American author who never undertook a formal study of Arabic culture and who, before writing the book, had never travelled to the Middle East. It certainly made *Dune*'s original editors unhappy – one reportedly asked Herbert why 'there's so much Muslim flavour'.[14]

Others, however, have pointed out the care and attention that Frank Herbert paid to his sources, arguing that Fremen culture is not simply a grab-bag of exotic-sounding names and terms but a painstakingly researched futuristic culture whose Arabic influence

'Nothing is true, everything is permitted'

APHORISM COMMONLY ASCRIBED TO HASAN-I SABBAH

is treated throughout with the appropriate respect.[15] According to Professor of Islamic History, Ali Karjoo-Ravary: 'Unlike many of his, or our, contemporaries, Herbert was willing to imagine a world that was not based on Western, Christian mythology . . . We should recognize Herbert for exploring Islam and religion without . . . reducing them to a cliché.'[16] Muslim scholar and *Dune* enthusiast Haris Durrani agrees: '*Dune* does not cheaply plagiarize from Muslim histories, ideas, and practices, but actively engages with them.'[17]

To list all the 'loanwords' that Herbert borrowed from Arabic would take much more space than we have here – those interested can find plenty of resources online, such as the exhaustive glossary penned by *Dune* enthusiast Khalid Baheyeldin.[18] But just a handful of the most notable are: *Sayyadina*, the Fremen name for a consecrated woman, taken from the Arabic word *sayyed* or master; *naib*, a member of a Fremen tribe and a word for deputy in Arabic; *shai hulud*, the Fremen name for the great sandworm, borrowed from two Arabic words: *shai* meaning thing, and *hulud* meaning eternal. Familiar Arabic words like *jihad, shariah, Hajj* and *Ramadan* all crop up in *Dune*, while landscape terms like *bled* and *erg* for parts of the desert and *qanat* meaning canal are all used by the Fremen and retain their original meanings.

But the Arabic influence on *Dune* is not merely present in the language. The appearance of the Fremen – hooded and robed, with only the eyes visible – recalls the desert garb of the Bedouin nomads of North Africa. Their religion, too, is named Zensunni, an ancient amalgamation of Zen Buddhism, Sunni Islam and countless other religions. And while Zensunni beliefs are common throughout the universe of *Dune*, they are particularly fervent among the Fremen, for whom religion has become more than just belief, but a unifying force and an emblem of rebellion.

That use of religion to bind people together may point the way to another Islamic figure whose mythic exploits might also have influenced Frank Herbert's creation of the Fremen. Hasan-i Sabbah – or, to give his full name, Hassan bin Ali bin Muhammad bin Ja'far bin al-Husayn bin Muhammad bin al-Sabbah al-Himyari[19] – was a scholar and a nation-builder, an Islamic missionary who founded the Nizari state of Ancient Persia.

Fathers of the Fremen: a member of the nomadic Bedouin or Bedu people

But he is perhaps best known as the instigator of a mysterious and enigmatic military organization: the Hashishin or Order of Assassins.[20]

Given that he was born in the year 1050, that copies of his autobiography no longer survive and that one of the most cited sources on his life is Marco Polo, who was born over a century after Hasan's death and dismissed him as 'a charlatan',[21] it is perhaps unsurprising that much of what historians know about Hasan-i Sabbah is steeped in rumour and myth. He apparently hailed from the city of Qom, now the seventh largest city in Iran, and was a self-taught student of astronomy, philosophy, languages and geometry. Taking on the role of a missionary within the branch of Shia Islam known as Isma'ilism, Hasan travelled to Cairo for study, but on his return was shipwrecked and had to be rescued off the coast of Syria. It was following this, in 1088, that he journeyed to the region surrounding the mountain fortress of Alamut near the Caspian Sea, where his legend would be forged.[22]

Remarkably, Hasan-i Sabbah is said to have taken control of the castle at Alamut without recourse to violence. Over two years, as the legend goes, he patiently converted the local populace, person by person and village by village, until finally he dispatched his followers to infiltrate and occupy the castle (other reports claim that he paid, or persuaded others to pay, large sums of money for the fortress). From Alamut, Hasan established the Isma'ilist state of Nizari – a network of fortresses and strongholds ranging throughout the local mountains, said to be oases of learning, civilization and wisdom. But Hasan could not hold his kingdom together by education alone. He needed his own warriors, his own *fidā'i* or Fedayeen, soldiers willing to carry out his orders even at the cost of their own lives.

From here, truth and legend become hopelessly entangled. Reasoning that it was less costly in both lives and money than open warfare, Hasan reportedly dispatched his followers to murder in secret those warlords and landowners who refused to join his new nation. Given that members of the Nizari nation had already been given the name

LEFT: Mythic hero Hasan-i Sabbah rides into battle

RIGHT: Knife of the assassin: Gustave Doré's 19th-century illustration depicts the attempted murder of King Edward I of England

Assassin, it wasn't long before the practice of murdering one's enemies and the popular name for those most notorious for doing so became intertwined.

Where, then, does hashish come into all this? Marco Polo claimed that the very word *assassin* was derived from *hashish*, and that Hasan would drug his followers, allowing them access to a walled garden that was the closest any of them would come to an earthly 'paradise', and to which only he could return them. This led to a belief that these warriors would smoke the drug as some kind of religious ritual, the better to bond them as a fighting force. However, some historians now argue that the term *hashish* is actually more likely to have been an insult levelled at the people of Nizari by their enemies – meaning 'low class', the word originally had no connection to the drug whose name it now shares.[23]

However complex the web of legend and history, it's easy to see how the legend of Hasan-i Sabbah might have sparked Frank Herbert's imagination. In the Order of Assassins we have a secretive band of religious warriors, bound together through the use of mind-altering substances and in thrall to a near-godlike leader, who has come from far away to grant them the gift of enlightenment and create a new paradise on Earth. At the time he was writing *Dune*, myths about the Hashishin weren't hard to come by, notably in Austrian historian Joseph von Hammer-Purgstall's dubious *The History of the Assassins*,[24] the novel *Alamut* by Slovenian writer Vladimir Bartol,[25] and in the works of William S. Burroughs, who had a lifelong fascination with the Hashishin and whose 1960 poem 'The Last Words of Hassan Sabbah' (sic) contains the immortal lines:

> *'And you, powers behind what filth deals consummated in what lavatory, To take what is not yours, To sell out your sons forever! To sell the ground from unborn feet forever.'*[26]

The Nizari state would endure beyond Hasan-i Sabbah's lifetime, while the notoriety of the Order of Assassins would continue to grow: they would be blamed for countless deaths in the coming centuries, from local emirs and sultans to European crusaders including the so-called King of Jerusalem, Conrad of Montferrat, in 1192. By the end of the thirteenth century, however, the Nizari state had been overwhelmed by Mongol invaders under the command of Kublai Khan, and the name of Hasan-i Sabbah would pass into legend.

But not all the influences on the Fremen are Arabic. At the age of 14, in the wilds near Burley, Frank Herbert had encountered a local man named Henry Martin – a member of the Hoh, part of the Native American tribe named the Quileute who are indigenous to

'Paul stood again before Stilgar, who said: "Now you are of the Ichwan Bedwine, our brother."'

FRANK HERBERT, DUNE [28]

the area. According to Herbert's son Brian, young Frank and the man he called 'Indian Henry' quickly 'became fast friends', the older man filling the boy's head with tribal knowledge including 'how to catch fish with your feet, how to poach fish, and how to identify edible and medicinal plants in the forest'.[27] The facts of this 'friendship' may never be known, but the image of a tribal elder taking a boy under his wing is central to *Dune*, as 15-year-old Paul Atreides learns the ways of the Fremen from his mentor, Stilgar. The encounter would also inform another of Herbert's novels, 1972's *Soul Catcher*, about a Native American man who befriends and later kidnaps the 13-year-old son of a prominent white politician as an act of revolution.

The Quileute people have been resident in the area now known as Washington State since long before the arrival of European settlers. Proficient boat-builders and fishermen, they also kept slaves from other tribes, harvested local trees to make tools and bred domesticated dogs for their fur. Indeed, Quileute folklore states that the tribe were themselves descended from wolves – a religious belief that author Stephenie Meyer took inspiration from when she cast the Quileute as a tribe of werewolves in her *Twilight* novels.

The first interactions between the Quileute and European invaders are assumed to have taken place sometime in the late eighteenth century, with reports of both peaceful trading and occasional fighting between Spanish sailors and local tribes. But it was in 1855 that relations were made – at least in the custom of the times – legal. The Quileute were persuaded to sign up to the Treaty of Olympia, whereby they ceded vast tracts of their land to the US government and agreed to live on a reservation at La Push, near Forks in Washington State.[29]

Henry Martin had spent much of his early life at La Push, as indeed had another of Herbert's major influences and closest friends, an environmentalist named Howard Hansen. Though not an official member of the Quileute nation, Hansen had been formally adopted by them (the question of his true parentage remains complicated, and

LEFT: Youthful wisdom: David Hudson was named chief of the Quileute tribe at just 11 years old

RIGHT: A 1979 edition of Frank Herbert's *Soul Catcher*

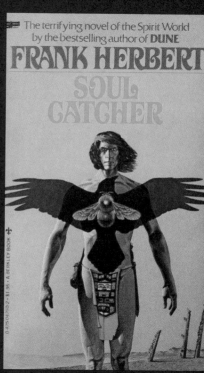

unanswered). He would meet Frank Herbert at a piano recital in Seattle soon after the war, and their friendship would prove an enduring one: Hansen was the best man at Frank and Beverly's wedding, and would be named as godfather to Frank's first-born son, Brian. But while Herbert would initially only dabble with ecological ideas – while at the same time working for conservative Senators and local logging interests – Hansen's views on the environment were shaped by his upbringing, and far more strident: 'White men are eating the earth,' he would reportedly tell Herbert, who only needed to look around him to recognize the truth of his friend's statement.[30] Indeed, the Fremen commitment to conservation and ecology has much more in common with the nature-focused beliefs of many Native American peoples than it does with most Arabic cultures.

But Hansen and the Quileute would lend more to Herbert than just an ecological perspective. In their small boats, the Quileute would regularly hunt whales off the coast of Washington, a show of extraordinary bravery that finds echoes in the way the Fremen use harpoon-like 'maker hooks' to conquer the great 'whale' of the desert, *shai hulud*. But perhaps more importantly, as Daniel Immerwahr observes in his essay on the relationships between Frank Herbert and First Nations peoples – 'The Quileute *Dune*' – it was from both Martin and Hansen that the author would acquire a perspective on the relationship between European settlers and First Nations people that was quite different from that of many of his contemporaries: this was, after all, the era of cowboys and Indians, of John Wayne and John Ford, of the Cleveland Indians, the Atlanta Braves and the Washington Redskins.

By honouring the struggles of tribal people against imperialist invaders in his fiction, Herbert proved that he was a writer ahead of his time – and by the late 1960s, this would help to make *Dune* feel unexpectedly contemporary. Indeed, the book would hit the first peak of its popularity just as many Native American people were joining the fight for civil rights, culminating in the 19-month occupation of Alcatraz Island from 1969 to 1971. And when, in March 1970, a similar protest took place closer to home, with the occupation of Seattle's Fort Lawton by members of the United Indians of All Tribes, Frank Herbert would take note, writing a sympathetic profile for the *Seattle Post-Intelligencer* of one of the movement's leaders, Bob Satiacum.[31]

In later *Dune* novels, the links between the Fremen and their Native American forebears become more complicated. When the warriors of Arrakis lose their connection to the desert they also lose their purpose and become 'museum Fremen', carrying out ancient rituals with no understanding of their meaning. It's hard not to see an arguably patronizing but surely well-meant reflection of the tragedy that overcame many Native American peoples following the theft of their land.

The Quileute themselves are now in a difficult position. The effects of climate change have made their land wetter rather than drier, causing devastating floods,[32] while over the past two centuries they have lost the knowledge of much of their culture and religion – the last original speaker of the unique Quileute language died in 1999. However, efforts are now underway to revive this extinct tongue, teaching it in the Quileute Tribal School and even offering audiobooks read in Quileute. Perhaps a Quileute edition of *Dune* might one day be produced, as a marker of the Native Americans' essential and still-echoing influence on Frank Herbert's life and work.

CHAPTER THREE
THE SPICE

The spice melange is the most valuable commodity in the *Dune* universe. Found only on the planet Arrakis, where it is a by-product of the life cycle of the indigenous Giant Sandworm, the spice is prized by the interstellar navigators of the Spacing Guild for its ability to give the user limited prescience, allowing them to plot a safe course across vast distances. Punishingly expensive and highly addictive, melange is also used in the consciousness-expanding rituals of the Bene Gesserit, and is stockpiled by the noble Houses of the Landsraad for its 'geriatric' or life-extending properties.

'Deep in the human unconscious is a pervasive need for a logical universe that makes sense. But the real universe is always one step beyond logic.'

SAYING ATTRIBUTED TO MUAD'DIB, *DUNE*[1]

On Arrakis, the spice permeates everything: mined from the sand and carried on the desert wind, it is also a staple of the Fremen diet. It is described as having a scent and a flavour redolent of cinnamon – another link back to the Arab world, for whom cinnamon is a common constituent of both savoury and sweet dishes. But the taste of melange is rather less predictable: it's never quite the same twice. As Dr Yueh tells Jessica: 'It's like life, it presents a different face each time you take it.'[2]

The metaphorical value of Herbert's spice is equally slippery. Most obviously, the significance of melange in the Imperium mirrors our current reliance on foreign oil. Just as petroleum – a resource mined in the desert and fought over by imperialist nations – is vital to our ability to travel, so the spice is key to navigation in space, which in turn makes Arrakis the lynchpin of galactic diplomacy. In the Imperium, trade in all commodities – spice included – is overseen by CHOAM, a corporation controlled by the Emperor and the noble Houses and inspired by the real-world consortium known as OPEC, or the Organization of the Petroleum Exporting Countries. We'll return to these resonances later, in a chapter dealing exclusively with CHOAM. For now, let's look at the spice itself: its purpose in the story of *Dune* and its effect on the heroes and villains of Herbert's universe.

In the early 1960s, when Frank Herbert was writing *Dune*, the drug lysergic acid diethylamide, known as LSD or acid, was not yet in common usage. Synthesized by Swiss chemist Albert Hoffman in 1938, the drug took time to filter through to the popular consciousness: though it would be used recreationally from the early 1960s, it wasn't until 1967, two years after *Dune*'s single-volume release, that the psychologist and 'acid guru' Timothy Leary would establish his League for Spiritual Discovery and kick off the psychedelic revolution in earnest.

But psychoactive substances and hallucinogens were far from unknown. Natural substances such as mescal beans, psilocybin or 'magic' mushrooms and peyote, derived from the cactus of the same name, had all been utilized for centuries in the

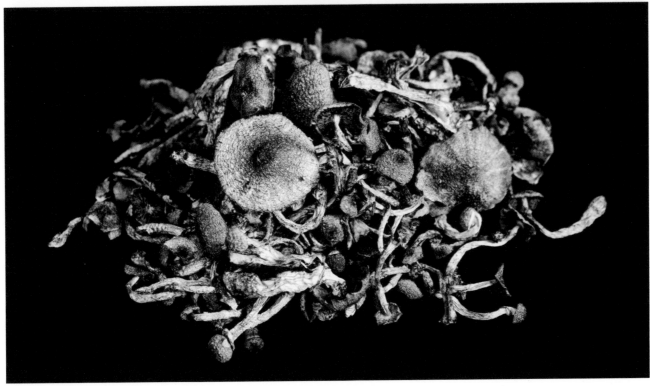

religious rituals of Native American and other First Nations tribespeople, from whom, as we've already seen, Frank Herbert had taken much of his inspiration. For the Fremen, the melange-derived Water of Life – or at least its 'transmuted' form, chemically altered by a shamanic Reverend Mother – occupies a similar function, allowing them to take part in 'sietch orgies' where, as Chani tells Paul, 'We're together – all of us. We . . . share. I can . . . sense the others with me'.[3]

For the hippies and psychic explorers of the 1960s, psychoactive drugs like LSD and peyote would, at least initially, perform the same duty: taken collectively, these substances would induce feelings of great unity and oneness. Once again, then, *Dune* arrived at precisely the right time: just as its sympathy with anti-imperialist rebels helped the book find favour with the radical anti-establishment, so its descriptions of drug-induced hallucinations lent the book huge currency within what would soon be termed the 'counter-culture'.

Not that Frank Herbert would necessarily embrace this aspect of his novel. Stating that 'I don't think drugs are the answer . . . people who come to rely on them begin to lose conciousness',[4] the author would publicly admit to having taken psychedelic substances only twice, both during his 1953 sojourn to Mexico and both by accident. First, he inadvertently consumed sweets laced with hashish and later he took a drink made from morning glory seeds.[5] Yet, while there's no concrete evidence of Herbert having ever sampled anything stronger, the noted mycologist Paul Stamets (himself an icon of the sci-fi community, having inspired the scientist of the same name in *Star Trek: Discovery*) would claim otherwise. Stamets wrote that he had discussed psychedelics with Herbert, who admitted that not only was the 'blue within blue' of Fremen eyes a nod to the blueish colour of psilocybin fungi, but that 'his [Herbert's] imagination was stimulated through his experiences with the use of magic mushrooms'.[6]

The truth of this claim is impossible to verify, but Herbert's professed lack of personal experience with psychoactive drugs didn't prevent him from exquisitely evoking the psychedelic experience in several passages throughout *Dune*. 'The poison drug had transformed her,' he writes of Jessica's experience after taking the Water of Life. 'She saw her own life as a pattern that had slowed and all life around her speeded up.'[7] When Paul himself drinks the Water, the echoes are even more powerful. As Jessica peers into her son's consciousness, she sees 'a region where a wind blew and sparks glared, where rings of light expanded and contracted, where rows of tumescent white shapes flowed under and over and under and around the lights, driven by darkness and a wind out of nowhere'.[8] As many of Herbert's readers would no doubt have said, 'far out'.

Another fascination Frank Herbert shared with the counter-culture, notably Leary himself, was with the untapped possibilities of the human mind and the expansion of our collective consciousness. From the late 1950s onward there had been much discussion on the wilder fringes of the scientific community about the potential long-term effects of these increasingly popular drugs. As articles like amateur mycologist R. Gordon Wasson's 1957 *Life* magazine piece 'Seeking the Magic Mushroom' wondered, could psychedelic fungi unlock pathways in the brain, offering new ways forward for humanity?[9]

For Herbert, the spice was his route to exploring these same ideas. Not only does melange allow the Reverend Mothers of the Bene Gesserit to unlock the past, opening a window into a great store of genetic memory, it also offers long-time users the chance to experience aspects of another of Frank Herbert's pet interests: extra-sensory perception or ESP – the ability to read minds and know the future.

Blue within blue: The unique colouration found in the eyes of a Fremen such as Chani (Zendaya), seen here in the 2021 film, is caused by long-term spice exposure

'Hope clouds observation'

BENE GESSERIT APHORISM, DUNE [10]

As a young man, Herbert had been intrigued, along with much of America, by the experiments carried out by Joseph Banks Rhine, the founder of parapsychology or the scientific study of psychic experiences and the paranormal. Born in Pennsylvania in 1895, Rhine could be both a believer and a sceptic – his declaration that popular medium Mina Crandon was a fraud led none other than Sherlock Holmes's creator and eager spiritualist Arthur Conan Doyle to post a notice in the Boston papers stating that 'J.B. Rhine is an Ass'.[11]

But by the 1930s, Rhine claimed to have discovered a strong scientific argument for the existence of ESP. Using symbol cards designed with his colleague Karl Zener, he developed a test whereby the scientist would attempt to 'project' an image into the mind of a willing subject (it's the same test Bill Murray conducts in the opening scenes of *Ghostbusters*, only without the electric shocks). When some participants scored significantly higher than the average, Rhine wrote his results up in a 1934 book, *Extra-Sensory Perception*, which would become an unexpected best-seller.[12] Over the coming years, thousands of amateur parapsychologists would repeat Rhine's experiments, though the scientific community would remain dubious. A 1936 study at Princeton utilizing 136 subjects and over 25,000 trials found that 'there is no evidence of extrasensory perception either in the "average man" or of the group investigated or in any particular individual of that group'.[13]

One willing believer, however, was young Frank Herbert, who carried out his own version of the Rhine experiment one night with a girl named Patty and a well-shuffled deck of 52 playing cards. According to Herbert, his date looked at each card in turn and he guessed every one correctly, until 'suddenly she threw the whole deck down on the hearth of the fireplace and said, "This scares me! I don't want to do this anymore!"'[14] Though he was open to the possibility that other factors besides ESP may have influenced his guesses – 'I'm not ruling out the fact that I may have seen . . . a reflection of [the cards] in her eyes, or something of that nature'[15] – the incident would spark a lifelong interest in the study of advanced mental powers that would reach its full flowering in the character of the prophet, Paul Atreides.

Paul's talent is not mind-reading, however, but prescience – the ability to see the future, as visionaries, mystics and charlatans have claimed to do since the dawn of time. For Herbert, part of the fascination of *Dune* was to imagine what would really happen to a living prophet, to someone with the genuine ability to see into the future: 'an examination of absolute prediction and its pitfalls.'[16]

TOP: The acid guru: Timothy Leary addresses the crowd at the Human Be-In festival in San Francisco, 1967

BOTTOM LEFT: J.B. Rhine, whose belief in ESP led him to write the 1934 book Extra-Sensory Perception

BOTTOM RIGHT: Zener cards, such as the ones Rhine utilised in his controversial ESP experiments

Part One: Arrakis

The result isn't pretty. For Paul, the gift of prophecy makes his life miserable. Throughout the second half of *Dune* he knows that a war is coming, a galactic conflagration whose fuse he will light and which will claim billions of lives. But he is powerless to prevent it because the wheel is already in motion, the damage has been done. Later, in *Dune Messiah*, Paul's prescience renders him even more impotent: there are no surprises anymore, and his efforts to steer the course of the jihad have proved fruitless. (It was this transformation of the first book's hero into at best a victim, at worst a monster, that so incensed Herbert's original publisher Joseph M. Campbell, leading him to turn down the chance to serialize the second book.)[17]

And while Paul's oracular abilities are inherent in him from birth – part of his genetic destiny as the Kwisatz Haderach or super-being – it is his contact with the spice that brings those abilities into full bloom, allowing him to view the shifting possibilities of time. But it takes practice for Paul to reach this point; initially his foresight is unpredictable, his grasp on the future unreliable: 'The prescience, he realized, was an illumination that incorporated the limits of what it revealed – at once a source of accuracy and meaningful error. A kind of Heisenberg indeterminacy intervened . . .'[18]

Here, Herbert was dropping the name of another thinker who would have been familiar to many of his contemporary readers.[19] The German theoretical physicist Werner Heisenberg had published his infamous uncertainty principle in 1927, was awarded the Nobel Prize in 1932 'for the creation of quantum mechanics', and died a decade or so after *Dune* was published, in 1976. Quantum mechanics is, of course, that intricate and baffling branch of physics that deals with the universe on a sub-atomic level, and Heisenberg was one of its foundational thinkers, along with his colleague Wolfgang Pauli and British mathematician Paul Dirac.

The discovery of quantum mechanics represented an earthquake in the field of physics, and it's easy to see why: at the sub-atomic level, Heisenberg argued, the accepted laws no longer seem to apply. 'The smallest units of matter are not physical objects in the ordinary sense,' he claimed in a lecture series that would later become the 1958 book *Physics and Philosophy: The Revolution in Modern Science*. 'They are forms, ideas which can be expressed unambiguously only in mathematical language.'[20]

One of the pillars of this new science, his uncertainty principle is fully understood only by other physicists, but the general idea is as follows: it is impossible to state with perfect accuracy the position and speed of any given particle in the universe, because the more we know of one factor, the less we can be sure of the others. The principle, essentially, transforms physics into extremely well-educated guesswork, a fact that initially infuriated more traditional thinkers such as Albert Einstein, who famously wrote in a letter to a fellow physicist that 'God does not play dice with the universe'.[21]

For Paul Atreides – the closest thing Herbert's universe has to a god, at least until the ascendance of his son, Leto – Heisenberg's uncertainty principle applies not to physical particles, but to the fabric of time. The more he knows of what is to come the less he is able to affect it, and the more he tries to affect it the less predictable the future becomes. Thus, he is trapped by his own gift, which, as it grows more powerful – showing him not just what lies ahead, but the past and wider present as well – begins inevitably to destroy him. Ultimately, Paul comes to realize that the only way out of this prophetic trap is death: an ignominious end for the Emperor of the Universe, and for the son and heir of one of the Imperium's most noble families.

PART TWO

CALDAZN

HOUSE ATREIDES

The Galactic Imperium of *Dune* may be rigid and monolithic, but the same cannot be said of the noble Houses within it. Varied in size, in wealth, in strength and in temperament, they range from the brutal sadists of House Harkonnen to their honourable and respected rivals, House Atreides of Caladan.

'I must rule with eye and claw – as the hawk among lesser birds'

DUKE LETO ATREIDES, *DUNE*[1]

For Duke Leto Atreides, known as Leto the Just, the loyalty of his people is won by respect, generosity and self-sacrifice; as he proves on Arrakis, human lives are more important to him than any amount of precious spice. But as his concubine Jessica recognizes, 'the Duke is really two men': one loving and compassionate, the other a fiercely practical and hard-headed ruler – 'cold, callous, demanding, selfish . . . as harsh and cruel as a winter wind'.[2] He's also a man imprisoned by circumstance, unable to evade the trap set for him by his enemies, his Emperor and the fates. Which is only appropriate, given the inspiration behind his character.

The name Atreides was derived from Atreus,[3] the family name of Agamemnon, hero of the Trojan Wars. It was Agamemnon who led the Greek forces against the city of Troy, holding together a jostling alliance of competitive, mistrustful warriors through the sheer authoritative force of his personality. He was also, wrote Homer, counted among the greatest of Greek fighters, a 'lion' in battle who killed hundreds of the enemy. Like Duke Leto, Agamemnon was bound by oaths of fealty, sworn to defend the honour of his family when his brother's wife, Helen, was abducted by the Trojans. The resulting campaign would take him many miles from his home, with the strong possibility that he might never return.

But, again like Leto, Agamemnon also has a ruthless side. His haughty demeanour provokes a conflict with Achilles that almost brings down the Greek army, just as the Duke's imperious nature sparks the jealous anger of the Emperor and the Harkonnens. And Agamemnon can be brutal, threatening the infant son of Odysseus when the latter refuses to fight for the Greeks, stoning his loyal lieutenant Palamedes on a false charge of treason and, according to some versions of the legend, even sacrificing his own daughter Iphigenia to appease the wrath of the goddess Artemis. Duke Leto is never so callous – he loves and fears for his son, Paul. But for both men, the demands of leadership force them to act in ways that may seem ruthless to others.

The name of the Atreides' ocean-rich home world, Caladan, is also derived from Greek – it's a play on Calydon,[4] an ancient metropolis on the banks of the River Evenus that was home to the ferocious Calydonian boar, sent by the goddess Artemis to punish the city and its rulers. However, the nobles of House Atreides prefer to test their wits against a different beast – the powerful Salusan bull. Indeed, Duke Leto's father, the Old Duke, was gored to death by one of these creatures, whose head still hangs in the palace on Caladan before being moved to the Atreides's dining room in Arrakeen. With his father's dried blood sealed upon its horns, the head is kept by Duke Leto as a constant reminder of a man he both respected and feared.

TOP LEFT: The ancient artefact known as the *Mask of Agamemnon*, discovered at Mycenae in 1876

TOP RIGHT: The 17th-century masterpiece *The Wrath of Achilles* by Peter Paul Rubens shows Agamemnon rising furiously from his throne

BOTTOM: The death of Agamemnon's daughter as depicted in the 17th-century artwork *The Sacrifice of Iphigenia* by Pierre Biard II

NEXT PAGE: The mythic beast of Calydon as seen in *The Calydonian Boar Hunt* by Peter Paul Rubens, c. 1611–12

'What a great beast it must have been to carry such a head'

SHADOUT MAPES, *DUNE*[5]

TOP: A medieval bullfight, from the 13th-century illuminated manuscript known as *The Fierce Bull That Was Tamed*

BOTTOM: A later bullfighting scene, from *Bullfighting at Sevilla, Spain* by Adolphe and Émile Rouargue, c. 1850

The tradition of bullfighting goes back to the very earliest days of Mediterranean civilization, where it plays a key role in the Mesopotamian poem known as the *Epic of Gilgamesh*, among the oldest surviving works of literature. Bullfighting, bull-jumping and the sacrifice of bulls were all regular practices for centuries, from Iran to Crete to the Roman games, but it was on the Iberian Peninsula that the familiar traditions of bullfighting became established.[6]

In medieval Spain, as on feudal Caladan, bullfighting was a tradition reserved almost exclusively for the wealthy; those who could afford to keep and train animals for sport. Among its many historical enthusiasts, perhaps the most notable was Charlemagne, King of the Franks and later Holy Roman Emperor, who ruled much of Europe during the eighth century. At that time, bullfighting was more akin to jousting: the toreador would ride a horse and carry a lance with which to impale his bovine opponent. But successful practitioners were afforded great respect, among them the storied eleventh century knight El Cid, one of Spain's national heroes.

It wasn't until the eighteenth century that the practice of fighting bulls on foot became established, utilizing both the *muleta* – the red flag to enrage the bull – and the *estoc* – a two-handed blade with a cruciform hilt. Many of the traditions of costume and stance that we associate with bullfighting today were established as late as the early twentieth century, most of them by the quintessential matador, Juan Belmonte, who pioneered the technique of standing firm and allowing the bull to approach.

In *Dune*, bullfighting is a symbol of hubris, of the Duke's determination to hold fast against a far more powerful and aggressive foe. But, just as his father was unable to resist the thrill of the bullfighting arena even at the cost of his life, so Duke Leto steps knowingly into the trap set for him by the Harkonnens, believing that by sheer will and personal strength he can withstand their attacks. Like the Old Duke, he is proven tragically wrong.

But while their name may be Greek and their sporting traditions Spanish, the architecture and physical surroundings of the Atreides evoke a very different landscape. With its stone castles and storm-tossed seas, the planet Caladan has a distinctly North European feel, which for Brian Herbert signposts the influence of another of his father's favourite writers: William Shakespeare.

'In *Dune*'s palaces,' Brian writes in a biography of his father entitled *Dreamer of Dune*, 'with their banquet halls and dark passageways, one gets a very similar feeling to the castles in which Shakespeare's characters brooded and schemed.'[7] He also compares the murderous plots and feuds carried out by *Dune*'s noble families – those 'plans within plans within plans'[8] that the Baron Harkonnen is so proud of – to the royal plots and struggles for succession found in Shakespeare's history plays, notably *Richard III,* another tale of a proud dynasty brought low by the machinations of a deformed and monstrous villain.

But the influence of Shakespeare is detectable in *Dune* from the outset. Just as a play such as *Romeo and Juliet* opens by telling us what we're about to witness:

> '*From forth the fatal loins of these two foes*
> *A pair of star-cross'd lovers take their life;*
> *Whose misadventured piteous overthrows*
> *Do with their death bury their parents' strife.*'[9]

TOP LEFT AND BOTTOM:
The cavernous halls of
Elsinore in the 1948 film
of *Hamlet*, directed by and
starring Laurence Olivier

TOP RIGHT: Shakespeare's
hero confronts his destiny
in *Macbeth, Banquo and the
Witches* by Henry Fuseli,
c. 1793

So *Dune*'s chapter headings will regularly 'spoil' for the reader as-yet unrevealed plot developments, such as the betrayal of Dr Yueh and the death of Duke Leto. Similarly, while Shakespeare's plays feature poetic soliloquys where the characters reveal their innermost thoughts to the audience, so Herbert employs a similar technique by voicing the intentions, doubts, hopes and fears of his characters, allowing a much richer insight for the reader.[10]

Shakespearian symbols crop up throughout Herbert's book, from the significance of signet rings originally found in *Hamlet* – another tale of royal feuds and courtly vengeance – to the storms that drive Paul and Jessica, and the characters from *The Tempest*, away from the civilized world and into unknown territory.

But it is the Scottish play, *Macbeth*, that perhaps most informs *Dune*. Both tell of a man who finds himself in possession of great and unchecked power only to discover that it corrupts everything around him, leaving a trail of misery, blood and death. Both stories are steeped in prophecy; just as Paul's arrival on Arrakis is foretold in tales planted by the Bene Gesserit Sisterhood, so Macbeth's ascension to the throne is predicted by a group of women – referred to as 'witches', 'weird' and 'sisters'. Both works feature a character called Duncan who dies too young, and both depict the descent into despair and depression of their hero, as he comes to recognize the futility of existence and his own inability to influence the future.

'A popular man arouses the jealousy of the powerful'

THUFIR HAWAT, DUNE[11]

But despite their essential decency, the Atreides are far from flawless heroes. As Frank Herbert would later compel his readers: 'Don't lose sight of the fact that House Atreides acts with the same arrogance toward "common folk" as do their enemies.'[12] Indeed, just as they are essentially European (or American) in appearance and custom, so does the Atreides' arrival on Arrakis resemble that of a colonial power assuming command of a 'native' outpost.

As we've already discussed, Herbert drew heavily on both Arabic and Native American sources to create his Fremen, and the initial dealings between the powerful Atreides and their desert-dwelling 'charges' closely parallels the historical relationship between European invaders and the native population of both the Middle East and North America – namely that the Atreides are in charge, and nothing the Fremen can do or say will change that. It's a point sharply made in the opening moments of the 2021 film adaptation of *Dune*, as Chani's voiceover asks, 'who will our next oppressors be?'[13]

Of course, compared to their predecessors, the Harkonnens, the Atreides are benevolent conquerors: they don't make slaves of the populace, they don't massacre Fremen for sport and the Duke prizes manpower over spice wealth. The Atreides are even willing to learn from the Fremen; the Duke sends his envoy, Duncan Idaho, as an ambassador into the sietches, where he learns desert-survival techniques, the proper use of a Fremen-made stillsuit and vital customs such as the respect Stilgar displays when, in an apparently offensive act, he spits on the table in front of Duke Leto.[14]

But the Atreides also have selfish reasons for wanting to win over these desert warriors. Thanks to Idaho, Duke Leto has begun to suspect the truth about the Fremen: that there are many more of them than has ever been suspected, and that they are fierce and seasoned fighters. So, while the Duke is willing to indulge their foreign traditions, he's also eager to exploit the Fremen as spice miners, as soldiers in his fight against the Harkonnen and even as a 'back door' to ensure his family's escape into the desert if things should take a bad turn.

Eventually, of course, Paul will give himself over to the Fremen, assuming a Fremen name and allowing their 'desert power' to sweep him to victory. But for the Duke and his retinue, the Fremen are primarily a tool to be used, not a tribe to join. As swordmaster Gurney Halleck reflects: 'They spoke of the "touch of the spicebrush" to mean a man had gone too native. And there was always a hint of distrust in the idea.'[15]

This relationship illustrates a fascinating conflict in Frank Herbert's depiction of imperialist power. Yes, the author was sympathetic to the plight of oppressed peoples. But he was also a white American of European extraction who had worked for Republican senators and an organization of timber lobbyists.[16] Perhaps the struggle of the Fremen against the forces of the Imperium represents a battle fought not just on the page, but within the mind and soul of Frank Herbert himself. And if so, it would find its ultimate expression in *Dune*'s essential character, one of the most complex and troubled heroes in science fiction.

Duke Leto Atreides (Oscar Isaac) with trusted advisors Thufir Hawat (Stephen McKinley Henderson) and Duncan Idaho (Jason Momoa) in 2021's *Dune*

CHAPTER FIVE
PAUL MUAD'DIB

In *Dune*, as the planetary ecologist Liet-Kynes lies dying in the desert, he receives a vision of his father Pardot Kynes, the imperial scientist who began the process of transforming Arrakis from a desert into a garden. In a moment of 'profound clarity' Liet hears his father's voice, speaking perhaps the key line in the entire *Dune* series: 'No more terrible disaster could befall your people than for them to fall into the hands of a Hero.'[1]

One of Frank Herbert's very first intentions with *Dune* was to explore the myth of the religious leader. 'I wanted to do a book about the messianic impulse in human society,' he would tell *The Environmentalist*, 'looking at why we follow the leader. Because, in my view . . . they ought to come with a warning on the package that they're dangerous to your health.'[2] To explore this question of how and why a messiah arises, Herbert would 'steep myself in comparative religions, in psychology and psychoanalysis, in the then current theories of history, linguistics, economics, politics and philosophy.'[3]

For the downtrodden Fremen, the arrival of Paul Atreides seems the answer to their oldest and most deeply held prayers. For Muad'dib himself, the assumption of the godhood seems the fulfilment of a lifelong destiny, the attainment of a righteous and holy power. For the planet Arrakis, Paul's coming seems the ultimate blessing, speeding the transformation of this parched desert world into a green and flourishing paradise. But in *Dune*, things are rarely as they seem.

The name his Fremen followers bestow upon Paul Atreides is *Mahdi:* the leader prophesied to come from elsewhere and through his actions, transform Arrakis. Like so much else in the book, the word is of Arabic derivation, literally meaning 'guided one' and referring to a spiritual leader whose arrival will signal the impending apocalypse, but who will restore true religion before the world finally ends. Over the centuries, the name has been optimistically applied to a number of Islamic leaders, one of whom was a direct influence on the character of Paul Atreides.[4]

Born in Sudan under combined Ottoman and Egyptian rule in 1844, Muhammad Ahmad bin Abd Allah, better known as Muhammad Ahmad, would as a young man depart from his family's traditional boat-building business and devote his life to studying Sunni Islam. He would ultimately earn the title of sheikh and assume leadership of the Samaniyya order, a branch of that deeply spiritual and ascetic wing of the Islamic faith known as Sufism. In 1881, as his following grew, Muhammad Ahmad declared himself to be the long-prophesied Mahdi, who many scholars already believed would arise from the ranks of the Samaniyya. Not all the local religious authorities supported his claim, but enough rallied to his side to make Ahmad a real threat to the government in Khartoum. And when the Governor General wrote to him, trying to buy him off, the self-proclaimed Mahdi replied: 'He who does not believe in me will be purified by the sword.'[5]

In the years that followed, Muhammad Ahmad's revolution spread across Sudan, uniting tribes of Muslims and non-Muslims against a common oppressor. In 1883, Mahdist fighters overwhelmed a heavily armed Egyptian force and took their modern weapons – rifles and bullets – for themselves. By this time, following an unrelated uprising in Egypt, the government in Khartoum had been replaced by a British force under the command of General Charles Gordon, but their attitude towards the Mahdists was no different from that of their forebears (again, we hear an echo of Chani's words about the Fremen and their oppressors). A force of 4,000 British troops was dispatched to tackle the Mahdists, but despite initial success they were soon forced to retreat.

Gordon took charge of Khartoum in 1884, but it was too late. When communication lines were severed by the Mahdists, he sent runners to Cairo to demand reinforcements. But Muhammad Ahmad's forces were drawing closer, and in April they laid siege to the city. Britain at last sent men to relieve Gordon, but again they arrived too late. In January 1885, one of Gordon's own officers opened the city gate and allowed the Mahdist forces in. The British garrison was slaughtered and Gordon himself was hacked to pieces, his head laid at the feet of the Mahdi, who ordered it to be placed in a tree, 'where all who passed it could look in disdain, children could throw stones at it and the hawks of the desert could sweep and circle above'.[6]

LEFT: An 1886 illustration of the Mahdi, Muhammad Ahmad, by an unknown artist

RIGHT: An artwork depicting the British Camel Rider Corps under General Gordon

'Here lies a toppled god,
His fall was not a small one.
We did but build his pedestal,
A narrow and a tall one.'

TLEILAXU EPIGRAM, *DUNE MESSIAH*[7]

'Most of the desert natives here are a superstitious lot'

LIET-KYNES, *DUNE*[8]

The site of Muhammad Ahmad's tomb, first in c. 1910 (top); followed by a more modern image of the rebuilt monument (bottom)

To the disappointment of his followers, however, the Mahdi did not prove immortal. Six months after the fall of Khartoum, as his forces continued to sweep through Sudan, Muhammad Ahmad contracted typhus and died. He was buried near the ruined city of Khartoum, though his grave would later be smashed to rubble by the British and his head, according to Winston Churchill, 'carried off . . . in a kerosene can as a trophy' by Lord Kitchener.[9] The tomb has since been rebuilt, however, as a tribute to a man who named himself a prophet.

Exactly where Herbert first learned of the Mahdi is uncertain. Most likely it was from A.E.W. Mason's best-selling adventure story *The Four Feathers*[10] – about a cowardly British officer who resigns his commission only to become caught up in the Mahdist uprising – or from one of its many screen adaptations, which tend to characterize the British colonial forces as plucky and heroic while the Mahdists are depicted as gabbling, brown-skinned desert demons. Such racist tropes were of course commonplace in the kind of adventure stories Frank Herbert would have grown up reading – indeed, the first story he ever wrote as a boy was entitled 'Adventures in Darkest Africa'.[11] They may also, consciously or otherwise, have played a part in the creation of the desert-dwelling Fremen and their colonial messiah, leading some to argue that *Dune* constitutes a 'white saviour' narrative.

Such narratives come in many forms, but the essential idea is always the same: someone (usually a man) of European heritage comes into contact with a 'primitive' non-white person or group and uses his advanced knowledge and/or technological skills to deliver his new allies from oppression and 'darkness'. Often, this hero will learn a lesson or two of his own in the process: tribal wisdom or survival skills that he can pass on to his fellow 'civilized' peoples.

The history of the 'white saviour' trope is long and problematic, from Daniel Defoe's *Robinson Crusoe* (1719) and the legend of Pocahontas to 'The White Man's Burden', an 1899 poem by Rudyard Kipling, the India-born British journalist and author of *The Jungle Book*. Inspired by America's colonial efforts in the Philippine Islands, the poem finds Kipling exhorting the US and other white imperialist powers to 'send forth the best ye breed', not for their own gain but for the benefit of the world's poorer, darker, less-refined peoples. Working himself up into a jingoistic fervour, he calls upon his fellow whites to wage 'the savage wars of peace' so that those unhappy natives – 'half devil and half child' – can be saved from their own worst excesses.[12]

In the years since, white saviours have continued to haunt our bookshelves and our cinema screens, from the garish racism of *A Man Called Horse* and *Indiana Jones and the Temple of Doom* to the liberal good intentions of *To Kill a Mockingbird* and *Dances with Wolves*. Conflicts over what does and doesn't constitute such a narrative continue to spark debate – Marvel Comics properties like *Doctor Strange* and *Iron Fist* have run into trouble for trading on lazy tropes about 'mystical' Asian societies, while 2018 Oscar-winner *Green Book* was denounced by, among others, the family of its real-life lead character, African American jazz pianist Don Shirley.[13]

It's easy to see how the story of Paul Atreides maps on to the established 'white saviour' template. Paul's origins are clearly European-influenced while the Fremen are described as 'tanned' and 'sinewy', steeped in tribal ritual and ancient custom. Paul learns their ways and even assumes their culture, while at the same time trying to 'educate' the Fremen in alternative methods of combat, morality and statecraft – with varying degrees of success.

However, some have argued that, while the basic outline of *Dune* may mirror the 'white saviour' template, Frank Herbert was so concerned with examining and unpicking that very same narrative that the result is something much more complex. For scholar Haris Durrani, *Dune* is 'more fascinating and subversive than a straight-up "white saviour" narrative',[14] partly because it continually questions and critiques the motives of its so-called hero, but also because Frank Herbert's depiction of the Fremen is so rich. 'It is so detailed and specific with its Islamic and MENA [Middle Eastern and North African] references,' Durrani writes. 'As a Dominican Pakistani Muslim kid, reading the *Dune* books was life changing. It was the first time I'd encountered a major speculative work that took Islam and colonialism seriously.'[15]

Of course, the 'white saviour' story with the deepest influence on *Dune* is not hard to pinpoint. Colonel T.E. Lawrence was a British Army officer and diplomat, author of the sweeping memoir *Seven Pillars of Wisdom* – which Herbert undoubtedly read[16] – and inspiration for one of the most highly regarded films ever made, *Lawrence of Arabia*, which had its Los Angeles premiere on 21 December 1962, and which Herbert would most likely have seen in San Francisco early the following year, as he was working on the first serialized section of *Dune*.

Thomas Edward Lawrence was born in Caernarvonshire in Wales in 1888, the illegitimate child of a nobleman, Sir Thomas Chapman, and a governess, Sarah Junner. The surname Lawrence came from Sarah's presumed father, another aristocrat who managed to impregnate one of his household staff. This chain of illegitimacy didn't stop young Thomas from reading history at Oxford University before going on to work as an archaeologist for the British Museum, where among other projects he helped to excavate the ancient capital of Carchemish in Syria. In early 1914, he also carried out a mapping project in the Negev Desert, now part of Israel, ostensibly for research purposes but actually on the instructions of the British Army.[17]

Formally admitted to the military following the outbreak of the First World War, Lawrence was seconded to the Arab Bureau in Cairo, where he could draw on his knowledge of the region and its people. By November of 1914, Britain and its allies were at war not only with Germany but with the Ottoman Empire; a dwindling but still formidable imperial power that had reigned over the Arabic-speaking regions of the

Hollywood blockbusters *Dances with Wolves* (top) and *Indiana Jones and The Temple of Doom* (bottom) both employ white saviour tropes

Chapter Five: Paul Muad'dib   83

'I wrote my will across the sky, in stars'

T.E. LAWRENCE[18]

Middle East for over six centuries. The Ottoman Empire was increasingly unstable – the Young Turk Revolution of 1908 had offered the promise of reform, resulting in a constitutional monarchy under the Sultan Mehmed V. But, following a brief period of neutrality, their entry into the war on the side of the central powers – the reasons for which are still hotly debated – would prove a disastrous one.

Not that it appeared that way at first. In February 1915, Britain sought to cripple the Ottoman Empire by seizing control of the Dardanelles Strait, a narrow waterway between the Mediterranean and the Sea of Marmara, blocking Turkish access from the Black Sea. The ensuing struggle for the Gallipoli peninsula would last for more than a year and claim some half a million lives, many of them soldiers conscripted from Australia and New Zealand. But it would be won by the Ottomans, who forced the attackers to retreat, delivering a crushing blow to the British-led forces and their maritime commander, First Lord of the Admiralty, Winston Churchill.

Having failed to smash the Ottoman Empire from without, British efforts turned to weakening it from within. Throughout 1915, word had spread of a growing Arabic nationalist movement led in part by Sharif Hussein bin Ali, the Emir of Mecca. He offered to stage an armed revolt against the Turkish forces in exchange for a British guarantee that, following the Ottoman Empire's defeat, they would support the formation of an independent Arabic state. The British agreed – at least in theory – and in 1916 Lawrence was dispatched to the Hejaz region of what is now Saudi Arabia, meeting not just with Hussein but with his sons Ali, Abdullah and Faisal, the latter of whom, Lawrence argued, was the man best placed to lead the coming uprising.[19]

Lawrence worked as an official liaison, persuading Faisal and Abdullah to coordinate their revolutionary efforts with British military movements in the region, and working with Faisal to plan the details of a widespread guerrilla campaign against the Ottoman forces, to be carried out largely by local Bedouin tribespeople. He also took part in a number of military actions, including the bombing of several positions along the Hejaz railway, Turkey's main route for troop movements.

In 1917, following the successful capture of the strategic coastal town of Aqaba by Faisal's forces in a sneak attack through the desert, Lawrence was granted a free hand by the British Army. 'He knew their language, their manners and their mentality,' his superior officer General Allenby would recall in a 1935 radio interview,[20] and indeed Lawrence would go on to adopt many local customs: photographs from the time show him in full desert garb, often seated astride a camel, gazing proudly into the dunes.

The Arab Revolt would suffer setbacks, but it's generally agreed that this desert uprising played a decisive role in driving Ottoman forces from the Middle East, leading to the capture of Damascus and ultimately to the Ottoman Empire's demise and dissolution. But the British had no intention of honouring the agreement they'd made with Hussein and his sons. Precisely when Lawrence became aware of this remains up for debate, but as early as 1915 the British, French and their allies had been working on the infamous Sykes–Picot Agreement, a secret treaty to divide significant parts of the Ottoman Empire between themselves, including the entire Middle East region.

So, while Faisal's campaign won him the right to rule over a democratic Syrian state, with elections held in May 1919, this independent nation lasted just over two years before French colonial forces took Damascus in 1920. By this time Lawrence had returned to England, where throughout the coming years he would speak on stages across the world about his experiences, penning two highly regarded memoirs and earning the grandiose title of Lawrence of Arabia.

LEFT: Sharif Hussein bin Ali and his supporters leaving his palace in Amman, Jordan, 1924

RIGHT: Saviour or 'shameless exhibitionist'? T.E. Lawrence in traditional desert robes, c. 1916

'He was a poet, a scholar and a mighty warrior. He was also the most shameless exhibitionist since Barnum and Bailey.'

THE 1962 FILM *LAWRENCE OF ARABIA*[21]

Completed in 1922 but not published until 1926, Lawrence's memoir, *Seven Pillars of Wisdom*, offers a riveting account of the Arab Revolt and his own role in it, based on the extensive notes he kept throughout the campaign. In the decades since, the book has been picked apart by scholars and biographers, its many truths and insights celebrated while its obfuscations and exaggerations have been exposed and debated. But the truth of Lawrence's book is largely irrelevant here, because the parallels between his story and that of Paul Atreides in *Dune* are self-evident.

Both are outsiders, dropped into a desert setting already rife with struggle between imperialist colonizers and 'native' nomads. Both are the sons of unwed parents; both hail from far-off, water-rich birthplaces. Both involve themselves deeply in tribal life – down to the level of dress and speech – and both end up taking charge, to a lesser or greater extent, of the ongoing revolt. Both form educational friendships with powerful men – for Lawrence, his friend and mentor, Faisal; for Paul, the Fremen leader, Stilgar – while offering moral and technological lessons of their own. But how much of Paul is drawn from the real-life Lawrence of *Seven Pillars*, and how much from the more glamorous figure portrayed by Peter O'Toole in the screen version?

For their biopic of Lawrence, screenwriters Michael Wilson and Robert Bolt and director David Lean took extensive liberties with the truth: *Lawrence of Arabia* may be a masterpiece of cinema, cited by no less an authority than Steven Spielberg as the reason he wanted to become a director,[22] but it should under no circumstances be mistaken for fact. Not only did Lean and his writers extensively reshuffle the timeline – the attack on Aqaba is depicted as Lawrence's first intrepid salvo in the campaign, and Faisal's efforts to build a consensus government are shown to last a single night rather than two years – but they also present Lawrence as the sole catalyst for the uprising, what Allenby called 'the mainspring of the Arab movement',[23] when in truth the Arab nationalist struggle had been gaining strength for at least a year before his arrival. (The contributions of several other European experts, liaisons and advisors – among them Lawrence's military companion S.F. Newcombe and writer and explorer Gertrude Bell – were also completely written out.)

No film biopic can ever be an exact rendering of events, but *Lawrence of Arabia*'s willingness to 'print the legend' is conspicuous. So as Frank Herbert worked to create

TOP: Prince Faisal (front) at the Paris Peace Conference in 1919, with T.E. Lawrence to his immediate left

BOTTOM: With his mentor Stilgar (Everett McGill), Paul Muad'dib (Kyle MacLachlan) prepares to ride the sandworm in 1984's *Dune*

NEXT PAGE: Director David Lean and his crew shoot a desert scene for 1962's *Lawrence of Arabia*

'He was warrior and mystic, ogre and saint, the fox and the innocent, chivalrous, ruthless, less than a god, more than a man'

PRINCESS IRULAN, *DUNE*[24]

a larger-than-life messiah figure for his novel, it's perhaps unsurprising that he would lean as much or more on the idealized, big-screen version of Lawrence as on his flawed and complicated real-life counterpart. In Lean's film, Lawrence is more than a mere mortal: gifted with the flawless features and ice-blue eyes of Peter O'Toole (who looks entirely unlike the real Lawrence), he appears as some sort of superhero, an impassioned soldier who can charm any man he meets, survive longer in the desert than his Arab counterparts and foresee victory as though speaking prophecy. It's a deeply persuasive depiction, and it seems to have worked its magic on Frank Herbert.

'If Lawrence of Arabia had died at the crucial moment,' he would tell Willis McNelly, 'he would have been deified. And it would have been the most terrifying thing the British had ever encountered, because the Arabs would have swept that entire peninsula.'[25] His implication is that the Arab uprising was only possible thanks to the intervention of Lawrence, and that only his death and martyrdom could have driven the Arabs to 'sweep the peninsula' and drive the British out.

But this reading doesn't reflect the reality of the situation. As demonstrated by Faisal's successful, albeit temporary creation of a Syrian democratic state, the rebels did not need a white man to lead them. It wasn't how Lawrence saw things, either: throughout *Seven Pillars of Wisdom* he examines his part in the Arab Revolt, writing in the book's introduction: 'Instead of being proud of what we did together, I was continually and bitterly ashamed.'[26] Later, he writes: 'Some of the evil of my tale may have been inherent in our circumstances. For years we lived anyhow with one another in the naked desert, under the indifferent heaven.'[27]

Paul Atreides may have moral concerns about his part in the violent jihad that he foresees, in the same way that the film version of Lawrence is dismayed when he and his Arab cohorts run down and massacre a phalanx of fleeing Ottoman troops. But, just as Lean's Lawrence marches straight into Faisal's tent and stakes his claim to command, so Paul never second-guesses his decision to become leader of the Fremen,

LEFT: The flawless features of Peter O'Toole as the title character in *Lawrence of Arabia*

RIGHT: Muad'dib and his Fremen followers in the 1984 film of *Dune*

while the Fremen themselves – from Stilgar on down – bow naturally to Paul, despite his youth and his inexperience. They will soon become 'his people'.

None of this, however, makes Paul an unblemished hero – at least, not for Frank Herbert. Just because Muad'dib is the messiah, the Mahdi, the Kwisatz Haderach, 'the universe's super-being', doesn't mean that his influence on the Fremen, on Arrakis or on the future of humanity itself is in any way positive. In fact, the opposite is true; as Herbert writes in *Dune*, the Fremen and indeed the wider galactic population are not saved or elevated by Paul's ascent to godhood, they are 'afflicted by a hero'.[28] In his essay 'Dune Genesis', he would go further: 'Beneath the hero's facade you will find a human being who makes human mistakes. Enormous problems arise when human mistakes are made on the grand scale available to a superhero.'[29]

Dune may seem at first like a heroic tale in the vein of Beowulf or *Beau Geste*, an epic story of derring-do in exotic lands. Paul may appear Christ-like in his powers of prophecy, his words of wisdom, his leadership of the Fremen to 'true freedom'. But these appearances are in fact undermined all the way through *Dune*, as Paul becomes ever more trapped by the future he can't avoid, and the jihad he longs to escape but ultimately gives himself over to.

In later books this idea is placed front and centre, as Paul transforms from the vengeful emperor of the universe – comparing himself to Genghis Khan and Hitler, only far worse – to a blind, helpless beggar, forcing his son Leto to spend thousands of years painstakingly attempting to undo his father's legacy. As Herbert himself would famously say: 'the difference between a hero and an anti-hero is where you stop the story.'[30] In *Dune*, he pauses at just the right point to make Paul appear noble, but in later books he would work hard to unpick that shallow mirage.

LADY JESSICA AND THE BENE GESSERIT

The place of women in *Dune* is a complicated one.
Frank Herbert's relationship with his wife Beverly seems
to have been the bedrock of his existence: she was his
first and most enthusiastic reader, he respected her
opinion in all things and even 'modelled Lady Jessica'
after her.[1] But, at the same time, he stood back while
Beverly set aside her own creative ambitions in order
to raise Frank's family and, at times, to work so that
he could write, giving him the time and space to indulge
his creative ambitions. As Herbert himself admitted:
'Bev . . . commuted to work and took care of the nitty
gritty of keeping us from starving to death.'[2]

In *Dune*, the roles of men and women are clearly defined: 'women remain the keepers of the dark mysteries,' Herbert wrote, 'and . . . men invade such matters at their own peril.'[3] From the noblest Great House to the lowest Fremen sietch this is a staunchly patriarchal society: the Padishah Emperor may respect his daughter Irulan, but there's never any question of her ascending to the throne. Similarly, while Liet-Kynes's daughter Chani may prove herself in battle alongside her Fremen brothers, she could never assume outright leadership of a tribe. In Harkonnen society, women are barely seen at all – the implication is that they are little more than chattels. Even among the Atreides, women are granted positions of respect rather than direct access to power: Duke Leto may hold Lady Jessica in the highest esteem as his concubine, his secretary, his business advisor and the mother of his only son, but when it comes to military matters and the leadership of his people, he stands alone.

This separation of gender roles would seem to mark *Dune* out as a product of its time, before the advent of any concerted women's liberation movement. But as with so much else in Frank Herbert's writing, first appearances can prove deceptive. Ahead of the release of the 2021 film adaptation of *Dune*, director Denis Villeneuve and actor Rebecca Ferguson made much of the fact that they'd 'expanded' the role of Lady Jessica: 'She's a mother, she's a concubine, she's a soldier,' Ferguson enthused.[4] But Jessica is already most of those things in Frank Herbert's book – and she's much more besides.

Her preternatural skills of observation allow Jessica to see the trap tightening around Duke Leto; they also give her the power to trick the Harkonnens into freeing Paul, allowing for an escape into the desert. Jessica may not be a 'soldier' in the literal sense, but her expertise in close combat enables her to overcome Stilgar, one of the mightiest of all Fremen warriors. Later she will become a Reverend Mother to the Fremen, a religious leader able to draw on the experiences of generations of women. And in fact, it is a decision made by Jessica that kickstarts the entire plot of *Dune*. Her choice to take charge of her own reproductive system and give birth to the son that Duke Leto longs for, rather than the daughter required of her by the Bene Gesserit Sisterhood, makes possible every event that follows. The fact that Jessica knows that Paul might grow up to be the fabled Kwisatz Haderach only makes her decision more potent and impactful.

For *Dune* scholar Kara Kennedy, this sense of purpose and self-possession makes Jessica a unique and formidable heroine. 'She is almost always in control . . . for a woman in science fiction, that is rare. She's so confident, because she's had all this training. And who gave her that training? An all-female Sisterhood.'[5]

Jessica may be among the strongest characters in *Dune*, but there's never any doubting the source of that strength: the Bene Gesserit Sisterhood, that murky, semi-religious school whose machinations have helped steer the course of galactic events for centuries. Here we find the other route open for women in Herbert's world: as secretive powerbrokers, whispering manipulators, the power behind the power. They may not be permitted to sit on the imperial throne, but they can pull the strings of the man who does.

Like much else in *Dune*, the real-world roots of the Bene Gesserit are endlessly tangled. Biographer Timothy O'Reilly argues that their earliest inspiration must have been Frank Herbert's own maternal aunts – a gang of powerful Irish Catholic women who 'overcame Herbert's agnostic father and insisted that the son receive Catholic training'.[6] He would be instructed in the ways of the faith by Jesuits, an order whose name bears an uncanny similarity to the word 'Gesserit' – indeed, Herbert himself would go on to describe the Bene Gesserit as 'female Jesuits'.[7]

Doting mother or galactic manipulator? Lady Jessica as played by Francesca Annis in the 1984 film of *Dune* (above) and by Rebecca Ferguson in the 2021 adaptation (right)

'The dark side of the magic universe belongs to the Bene Gesserit'

TYLWYTH WAFF, *CHAPTERHOUSE: DUNE*[8]

LEFT: The power behind the
Imperial throne: Reverend
Mother Gaius Helen Mohiam
(Charlotte Rampling) in
2021's *Dune*

RIGHT: Divine inspiration:
*The Vision of Ignatius of
Loyola at La Storta in 1537*
by unnamed artist, c. 1622

The Jesuit order, or Society of Jesus, was founded in 1540 by Spanish minor nobleman and warrior Ignatius of Loyola, later canonised as Saint Ignatius. After his leg was shattered by a cannonball at the Battle of Pamplona, Ignatius dedicated himself to religious work and set out on a pilgrimage to the Holy Land. At the same time, he claimed to have received a series of religious visions that would ultimately lead to the founding of a new Roman Catholic order, based in Paris and dedicated to spreading the gospel throughout the world. The Society of Jesus would become one of the most widespread and influential of all Catholic orders.

Already we can see clear parallels with the Bene Gesserit: as Kara Kennedy observes, the two are united by 'their commitment to service, missionary programmes, education system, and political influence'.[9] While the missionaries of the Society of Jesus dedicated themselves to spreading the Christian gospel across the globe – often to the detriment of indigenous peoples – in *Dune* it's the Bene Gesserit's Missionaria Protectiva who are responsible for sowing the seeds of religious superstition and prophecy among the galaxy's more marginal cultures. But the Jesuits exerted a powerful political influence too, acting as confessors and advisors to many of the most powerful ruling families in Europe. Similarly, Bene Gesserit sisters such as Reverend Mother Gaius Helen Mohiam and the Lady Jessica act as confidantes and counsellors to men of power, including the Padishah Emperor himself.

Also notable is the fact that one of the key religious texts for the Bene Gesserit, and indeed in the Imperium as a whole, is entitled the Orange Catholic Bible. However, despite its name, the OCB isn't a purely Catholic text – as we learn in *Dune*'s appendices, it's actually a compendium of all religious thought, a pantheistic scripture created during a great meeting of religious leaders centuries ago on Old Earth, known as the Commission of Ecumenical Translators. The OCB combines 'elements of most ancient religions, including the Maometh Saari, Mahayana Christianity, Zensunni Catholicism and Buddislamic traditions'.[10] Once again, the feverish complexity of Herbert's imagined universe serves to undercut simple interpretations.

Another possible source for the name Bene Gesserit is a Latin phrase meaning 'well behaved' – as in the legal phrase *quamdiu se bene gesserit* (or *gesserint*), which states that a person shall be allowed to hold a particular office for as long as she conducts herself properly – while a third option is that the name may have been taken once again from Arabic, where *beni* means 'sons' or 'children of', while Gesserit could be a corruption of *jazeera*, meaning 'island' or 'peninsula', the same word from which the global news channel Al Jazeera takes its name. The simplest likelihood, of course, is that Herbert was aware of all three, and enjoyed the linguistic similarity.

What isn't in doubt are the inspirations behind the Sisterhood's remarkable powers. Chief among these is the Voice, that technique of precisely pitching the tone of one's speech in order to control and manipulate a weaker-minded being. Here, Herbert was influenced by his study of general semantics, a philosophy of language developed in the early twentieth century to explore how words affect our perception of the world, and how the names we give to things can influence our experience of those things.

General semantics was first developed in the early twentieth century by Polish thinker Alfred Korzybski, and further defined in his 1933 book *Science and Sanity: An Introduction to Non-Aristotelian Systems and General Semantics*.[11] Korzybski recognized that our perception of the world is heavily influenced both by our physical body, whose sensations constantly bombard us, and by language, the limitations of which can restrict how much we are capable of understanding. As a result, we often 'misread' reality – a tendency that Korzybski was determined to stamp out. Through general semantics, he claimed, humanity would be able to recognize its own limitations and thereby overcome them, gaining a richer understanding of what is really happening around us.

One anecdotal example of Korzybski's technique occurred during a lecture he was giving. Claiming to be ravenously hungry, Korzybski opened a packet of biscuits and ate two before offering the rest to his students, remarking enthusiastically on how delicious they were. Once they'd finished eating, Korzybski tore back the packet to reveal that they'd been consuming dog biscuits – causing two of the students to vomit on the spot. 'You see,' Korzybski told them, 'I've demonstrated that people don't just eat food, but also words.'[12]

Among Korzybski's most distinguished students was a man who would go on to popularize the study of general semantics: Samuel Ichiye Hayakawa. Born in Canada of Japanese descent, Hayakawa worked as a professor of English and later President of San Francisco State University before running successfully as a Republican Senator and serving the state of California from 1977 to 1983. First published in 1949, his million-selling book *Language in Thought and Action*[13] was written for a wide audience and was intended not just as a study of general semantics but a handbook to enable readers to recognize how their perceptions are shaped by the words they use. Around the time he was researching and writing *Dune*, Frank Herbert would encounter Hayakawa in person, working briefly for the then-professor as a ghost writer. Fascinated by the principles of general semantics, he would read both Hayakawa and Korzybski's work thoroughly, weaving their ideas throughout *Dune*.

In the future Herbert envisioned, general semantics has been developed to the point where humans can be trained to be completely aware of the words they and others utilize, and the layers of inference and meaning hidden within them. Hayakawa called these 'metamessages' – the underlying meanings beneath the words. In *Dune*, language is merely the surface – the Atreides family have their own 'battle language', a series of code words to warn each other of danger without allowing others to become aware of

Frank Herbert was a keen
student of the principles
of general semantics as
defined by Samuel Ichiye
Hayakawa (left) and
Alfred Korzybski (right)

it, while the Bene Gesserit use their extraordinary powers of observation to detect the hidden meanings in seemingly ordinary conversations. By paying complete attention to the way a person speaks, the words they choose and the stresses they place on them, a trained Sister can read that person's emotional state, their personal history, even their intentions, good or bad. Here we see the influence of another writer whose work would surely have been familiar to Herbert: Arthur Conan Doyle. In their absolute attention to detail and their razor-sharp levels of observation, the Bene Gesserit are surely the many-generations-removed successors to that great detective, Sherlock Holmes.

But the ultimate expression of Bene Gesserit power is the Voice. In filmed versions of *Dune*, the Voice tends to be depicted as a magic spell cast upon a weaker-minded opponent, a kind of 'Jedi mind-trick'. But for Frank Herbert, it was something far subtler. The user of the Voice minutely observes the person they wish to manipulate, and modulates their speech accordingly, choosing the exact pitch, timbre and words to sway that person's feelings and drive them to act.

Herbert would later explain his thinking, taking the blunt caricature of a loyal soldier, a small-town American patriot and conservative. It wouldn't take much, the author argued, just a few well-chosen words to influence this man's emotions and make him hopping mad. 'If you know the individual well enough,' Herbert argued, 'if you know the subtleties of his strengths and weaknesses, then merely by the way you cast your voice, by the words you select . . . you can control him.'[14]

'Life is not a problem to be solved, but a reality to be experienced'

J.J. VAN DER LEEUW, BORROWED FOR *DUNE*[15]

The Voice is a far more advanced practice than simply pushing someone's emotional and political buttons, but the essential idea is the same. It all comes back to general semantics, developed over millennia into a fine art, and even a weapon. It's a truth that the Atreides' Master of Assassins Thufir Hawat learns when he challenges the Lady Jessica: 'His body had obeyed her before he could think about it,' Herbert writes. 'To do what she had done spoke of a sensitive, intimate knowledge of the person thus commanded, a depth of control he had not dreamed possible.'[16]

But the Bene Gesserit practice of enhanced awareness isn't limited to words and language. The Sisterhood also practises an art known as *prana–bindu*, the total comprehension and control of one's body: organs, nerves and muscles. Its name taken from Sanskrit, where it means 'energy points', this ultimate mind-body discipline again sees Herbert taking real-world ideas and developing them, imagining how they might become exponentially more formidable in the future. With *prana-bindu* many of the ideas stem from Zen Buddhism, with its focus on mindfulness, and from yoga, with its emphasis on the body. Both of these practices might be familiar today, but in the early 1960s, when Herbert was writing, Eastern philosophy was not as fashionable as it would become in the wake of The Beatles' visit to India. Practitioners of meditation and yoga were few and far between – though perhaps less so in San Francisco.

Among those who encouraged Frank Herbert's interest in Buddhist beliefs was one of the men responsible for popularizing ideas of Eastern mysticism in the US: the English-born writer and 'philosophical entertainer', Alan Watts. Born in 1915 in the leafy environs of Chislehurst in Kent, Watts had developed an early fascination with Chinese culture, becoming secretary of the London Buddhist Lodge at just 16. Over the following decade he would explore Zen philosophy in New York, before leaving to study Christian theology in Illinois – a pair of very different traditions that Watts hoped to find a way to reconcile.[17] Moving to San Francisco in the early 1950s, he would spend the next decade studying everything from Japanese primitivist art to Chinese brush calligraphy, while at the same time publishing a number of books and essays on spiritualism and philosophy and hosting a long-running radio show discussing the impact of Eastern ideas on Western culture.

Herbert would cross paths with Watts in the early 1960s, after requesting an interview for his then-employer, the *San Francisco Examiner*. The two men 'were charmed by one another's company, and became friends',[18] engaging in hours-long conversations over a series of dinners, either at the Herbert home or on Watts's houseboat, the *Sausalito*. According to Brian Herbert, it was around this time that his father became a committed 'Orientalist', bringing home Japanese furniture, studying the *I Ching* and the haiku, stocking the family fridge with 'oriental herbs, tofu and beef tongue', and even referring to Brian as 'number one son' in the Japanese fashion.[19] He would also throw himself into research, studying everything Alan Watts had published and grilling the man for his thoughts on philosophy and mindfulness.

However, one area of study that would inform the Bene Gesserit is far more problematic and troubling. In *Dune*, the Sisterhood has been working for generations to produce a superhuman being, the Kwisatz Haderach. This time the name comes from Hebrew and is a corruption of the words *Kefitzat Haderech*, meaning a contraction of the road or a sudden leap between two places.[20] To create this long-awaited superman, they have engaged for millennia in a process of genetic manipulation, working to 'breed out' certain traits and 'breed in' others, controlling reproduction among the Great Houses.

When Frank Herbert was writing *Dune* the study of eugenics was already highly controversial, and it has only become more so since. The idea of selectively breeding human beings to preserve or enhance certain supposedly beneficial genetic traits goes back to the ancient Greeks; indeed the term is derived from the ancient Greek *eugenes*, meaning good or noble stock. Some form of eugenics has been practised throughout history – famously, the Spartans would inspect every child born to decide if it was fit to live in their society, while Roman parents were obliged to murder any child born with 'dreadful deformities'.

But it was the British scientist Francis Galton who coined the term eugenics, and who first codified it as a science. Inspired by his cousin Charles Darwin's theory of evolution, Galton began to research human characteristics, collecting data regarding height, fingerprints and so-called 'mental acuity'. He studied the lives and relatives of eminent men to discover if there was any basis to assume that human ability could be passed on, publishing the results in his 1869 book *Hereditary Genius*.[21] He proposed encouraging those with such traits to have more children, while those he deemed genetically 'weak' he suggested isolating in monasteries and sisterhoods to ensure their celibacy. His claim that 'there exists a sentiment, for the most part quite unreasonable, against the gradual extinction of an inferior race' is viewed by the editors of the *Encyclopaedia of Genocide* as 'close to justifying genocide'.[22]

By the turn of the twentieth century, Galton's ideas were already spreading insidiously. In America, the eugenics movement used his arguments to justify racial segregation while also suggesting that immigrants from so-called 'inferior' races, including Jews, should be limited. From Sweden to Japan, the enforced sterilization of those deemed 'mentally inferior' was carried out during the 1920s and 1930s.[23] But Galton would not live to see the full, horrific flourishing of his ideas.

In 1930s Germany, the prominent Nazi geneticist Ernst Rudin and others formed the Expert Committee on Questions of Population and Racial Policy, to address the question

'Even dangerous facts are valuable if you've been trained to deal with them'

DUKE LETO ATREIDES, *DUNE*[24]

of so-called 'racial hygiene', using the theory of eugenics as a pretext for murdering millions of 'undesirable' people and sterilizing many more. It was Rudin who emphasized 'the value of eliminating young children of clearly inferior quality', and his work would win him the Goethe Medal for Art and Science, to be placed in his hands by Adolf Hitler himself. Briefly interned by the Americans after the war, he would be released upon payment of a fine of 500 Reichsmarks.

In the wake of the Holocaust, enthusiasm for eugenics began to dwindle – indeed, many of its practices were deemed by international law to fall under the heading of genocide. But it never went away, particularly in science fiction: from *Brave New World* to *Gattaca,* sci-fi creators have always loved to explore the idea of genetic tinkering.

In the *Dune* saga, eugenics is taken as scientific fact – indeed, the Bene Gesserit breeding programme is only the first such project we encounter: later, the God Emperor Leto II will continue what the Sisterhood started, selectively breeding his own ancestors to produce a human being invisible to those with the gift of prescience. The books also employ dubious terms like 'racial stagnation' and 'race consciousness', proposing that humanity has to engage in violence to avoid becoming genetically 'weaker', while the Gom Jabbar Test that Paul undergoes in the very first scenes of *Dune* is meant to separate true humans from lower-status 'animals' in human form.

Dune's acceptance of eugenics as fact is one of the reasons why the book has become a favourite among those who hold extreme right-wing views. Modern 'geek fascists'[25] see Herbert's invention of a selective breeding programme to create a genetic 'superman' as compatible with their prejudicial ideas about race, and their unscientific belief in the inherent superiority of one inherited trait – e.g. skin colour – over another. They thrill to Herbert's vision of a messiah with European heritage staking a natural claim for leadership over the diverse peoples of the Imperium.

But these extremists conveniently overlook (or simply don't understand) those aspects of *Dune* that make the book wholly contradictory to their views. There's the fact that Muad'dib is far from a flawless genetic specimen: he's a self-described monster whose arrival is nothing less than a disaster for humanity. There's Frank Herbert's own veneration of non-white cultures and peoples, from those of the Pacific Northwest to the Middle East. And, of course, there's the unequivocally Arabic roots of the Fremen, one of whom will become the mother of Paul's heir, the even more powerful God Emperor, while Paul himself is secretly the product not only of the 'pure' Atreides but also their monstrous, parasitic and, yes, fascistic enemies – the most vile creatures in the known universe.

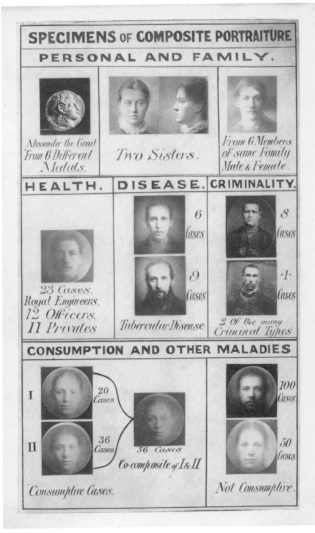

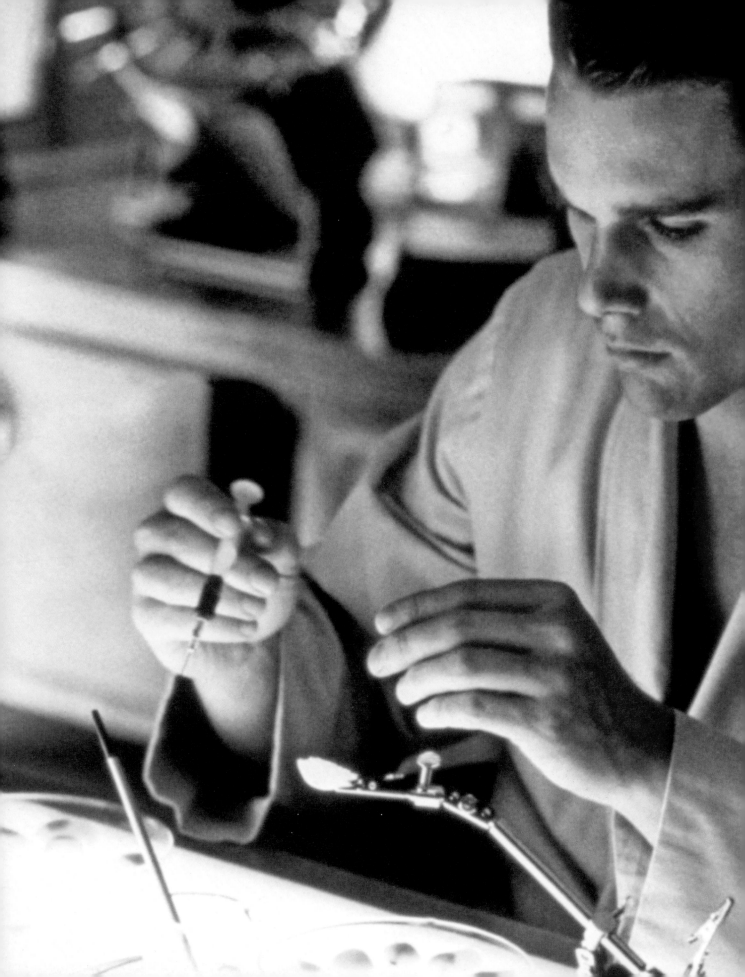

PART THREE

HOUSE HARKONNEN

Man or monster? A Roman
bust of the infamous
Emperor Caligula

If, as Muad'dib states, the Atreides home planet
Caladan is 'a paradise for our form of life',¹ then
hell must be the Harkonnen world of Giedi Prime,
an industrial labyrinth where millions toil beneath the
brutal yoke of a monstrous and corrupt ruling class.

Descriptions of this planet are scant in *Dune* – we read of puddled streets littered with rubbish and 'furtive scurrying' inhabitants;[2] we know there are vast factories, castles and arenas where the aristocracy engage in rigged gladiatorial battles. But it's not until thousands of years later, in *Heretics of Dune*, that we get a better sense of the planet as it was, now renamed Gammu. The entire world has been extensively replanted, but evidence of its mechanized past remains in the oil-soaked soil and huge, 950-storey rectangular structures – 'forty-five kilometres long, thirty kilometres wide' – that once housed Harkonnen cities.[3]

The bitter feud between House Harkonnen and House Atreides goes back 10,000 years, to the time when 'an Atreides had a Harkonnen banished for cowardice after the Batttle of Corrin'.[4] But while these two Great Houses may be moral opposites, the inspirations behind them are – at least in terms of geography and historical period – almost neighbours. Just as the culture of the Atreides was founded on that of ancient Greece, so Harkonnen society is clearly modelled on that of classical Rome – or at least its most degenerate, iniquitous aspects. Like the Romans, the Harkonnens invade and occupy far-off places and subjugate the native inhabitants; like the Romans, they build vast amphitheatres where highly trained fighters kill for entertainment.

Their ruler, the Siridar Baron Vladimir Harkonnen, is not just the most repulsive character in *Dune*, but one of the most hideous villains in all of literature. Morbidly obese and sexually voracious, the Baron has no checks on his power besides the Emperor and is consequently free to indulge every whim, however vile. If he has a real-world antecedent, then, it must surely be that byword for depraved dictatorship, the Roman Emperor Caligula.

Born Gaius Julius Caesar Augustus Germanicus in the year AD 12 and nicknamed Caligula or 'little boot' as a boy, the emperor would become infamous for the methods he employed to enhance and maintain his personal power. Modern historians have argued that many of the sources for Caligula's more extreme acts are less than reliable, with reasons of their own for slandering him, but that's beside the point. The very name Caligula has become synonymous with debauchery and political corruption, and that is how Frank Herbert would have known him.

Though he would rule as emperor for only four years (AD 37–41), the list of Caligula's supposed malfeasances is too long to list here. He was accused of widespread fornication with countless women, many of them the wives of his allies, and of incestuous relationships with his three sisters, whose sexual services he also allegedly sold to wealthy men. He spent vast sums on petty projects while thousands starved, and he tortured men, even high-ranking senators, by forcing them to run in front of his chariot. He killed for his own amusement, ordered countless executions and, according to his biographer Suetonius, the emperor's favourite phrase was, 'remember that I have the right to do anything to anybody':[5] words that might have come straight from the slobbering mouth of Baron Harkonnen himself.

But there's another, more problematic link between the Baron and his most significant Roman forebear: their profligate, predatory and incestuous sexuality. In the Baron's case, this is depicted as being strictly homosexual and often paedophilic in nature. He may once have been seduced by a member of the Bene Gesserit, resulting in the birth of his daughter, Jessica, but in *Dune* his preference for young boys is clearly stated. He orders his victims to be drugged – 'I don't feel like wrestling'[6] – and even kills one of his conquests, albeit for trying to poison him. Objects of his perverse lust include his own nephew, Feyd-Rautha, and his pubescent grandson, Paul Atreides.

'*What do you despise?*
By this are you truly known.'

PRINCESS IRULAN, *DUNE*[7]

Conflating homosexuality with predacious paedophilia remains a homophobic tactic right up to the present day, while depicting (and dismissing) corrupt officials as homosexual has a long history. Take the film *Lawrence of Arabia*, which glosses over T.E. Lawrence's own complicated sexuality while depicting with grim fascination his sexualized assault at the hands of a brutal Turkish general.

With *Dune*, however, the issue is complicated further by the fact that Frank Herbert's second son Bruce was himself gay. As described in his brother Brian's book, Bruce had a complicated relationship with his father from a young age. In his teenage years, when *Dune* was being written, the two were often at each other's throats, and Bruce would later leave home and move into what Brian refers to as a 'drug house'.[8] It can't have helped that Frank Herbert viewed homosexuality as 'an immature, unseemly activity',[9] writing in *God Emperor of Dune* that 'it's perfectly normal for adolescent females as well as males to have feelings of physical attraction toward members of their own sex. Most of them grow out of it'.[10]

Of course, Frank Herbert hailed from a generation for whom homophobia was par for the course – gay men and women were viewed as deviant, self-indulgent, even dangerous. But given his boundless imagination and voracious capacity for learning, it's perhaps disappointing that Frank Herbert doesn't seem to have applied his customary intellectual open-mindedness to his own son's lived experience.

Bruce Herbert would go on to become a respected photographer and a committed advocate for gay rights in San Francisco. Eventually, he was even able to be open with his family about his sexuality, going so far as to bring a boyfriend to the premiere of the 1984 film adaptation of *Dune*.[11] What the young couple made of Kenneth McMillan's diseased, slave-murdering Baron Harkonnen remains undocumented.

Another influence on the Harkonnen clan would have been instantly detectable to *Dune*'s original readers. The Baron's first name, Vladimir, can of course evoke only one culture, while according to Brian the name Harkonnen was selected by his father from the San Francisco phone book because it 'sounded Soviet'[12] (it's actually Finnish, and properly spelled Härkönen). This use of Russian or Russian-sounding names intentionally invokes the Cold War, at the height of which *Dune* was written, and suggests a relationship between the Atreides and the Harkonnen echoing that of America and Russia in the post-Second World War period. (The impression is intensified by our brief exposure to a group of Atreides soldiers, who talk uncannily like American GIs: '"No showers down here. You scrub your ass with sand!" "Hey, can it! The Duke!"')[13]

Like the Cold War, the rivalry between Harkonnen and Atreides has endured for many years, but it has never erupted into outright conflict. Both sides possess atomic weapons, even though their usage is strictly prohibited both by the Great Convention of the Landsraad and by moral consensus. The depiction of Giedi Prime as a murky, rubbish-strewn hellscape resembles many Americans' contemporary view of the Soviet Union, as a place where 'personal freedoms' were strictly limited and one's only loyalty was to the state and its rulers. We might even detect a hint of patriotism creeping into Frank Herbert's writing, a touch of pride in his own country and its stated dedication to the cause of freedom.

Among the Russian stereotypes familiar to Americans in this period would have been the muscle-bound thug, from bit-part heavies in James Bond films to the Soviet ambassador in 1964's *Dr Strangelove*. In *Dune*, this cliché is reflected in the character of the Baron's nephew, Glossu 'the Beast' Rabban, a 'muscle-minded tank-brain',[14] according to his uncle. Too stupid to comprehend the Baron's plans, he is dispatched to Arrakis as a blunt instrument, ordered to 'squeeze' the conquered planet for every ounce of spice, to brutalize its population and to exterminate the Fremen.

His brother Feyd-Rautha, meanwhile, is a far more subtle villain. In many ways he is presented by Herbert as a dark mirror to Paul Atreides: another aristocratic teenager, another trained fighter, another by-product of the Bene Gesserit breeding programme. But Feyd is a born schemer, risking his own life in the arena in an attempt to win over the rank and file and attempting to kill the Baron and take his throne. Unlike Paul, for whom stillness and self-control are paramount, Feyd is rash and psychotic, twisted by his upbringing at the hands of an uncle who forces him to 'kill all the women in the pleasure wing'[15] just to teach Feyd a lesson.

Where Feyd-Rautha comes closest to outstripping Paul is in the arena of one-on-one combat. In *Dune*, the widespread use of personal body shields has made long-distance weapons very dangerous: though laser weapons or 'lasguns' do exist, if their beam makes contact with a body shield, the resulting explosion is liable to eliminate both the target and the assassin. As a consequence, close-quarter combat has become normalized both on the battlefield – where large-scale battles using knives and swords recall the melee combat of medieval Europe – and in grand fighting arenas.

Like many other aspects of life in the Imperium, this combat has become deeply formalized and ceremonial. From the Fremen sietch to the amphitheatre on Giedi Prime, combatants observe strict codes of conduct, as taught to Paul by his father's swordmaster, Gurney Halleck. The Harkonnens, of course, use whatever means they can to circumvent these conventions: Feyd-Rautha may have killed 100 gladiators by his 15th birthday, but all were either drugged or brainwashed to weaken at the mention of a specific word.

In its rigidly formal nature, combat in *Dune* echoes both the gladiatorial battles of Rome – where those who were about to die would turn and salute the emperor – and also the martial arts of the Far East. Frank Herbert drew on his research into Zen Buddhism to create the Weirding Way, a form of hand-to-hand combat requiring total self-awareness – the aforementioned principles of *prana-bindu* – to give the combatant almost supernatural speed and agility.

Developed by the Bene Gesserit and taught by Paul and Jessica to the Fremen, the Weirding Way has parallels with the Eastern martial arts that were becoming increasingly popular in the US at the time, namely karate and judo (Bruce Lee would first appear on American televisions in *The Green Hornet*[16] not long after *Dune*'s publication, in 1966). But it is perhaps more interesting for what it – and the entire nature of hand-to-hand combat in *Dune* – represents.

As biographer Timothy O'Reilly writes, 'hand-to-hand combat underlines Herbert's emphasis on self-reliance and personal skill'.[17] The impossibility of long-range warfare, the outlawing of atomics and the restriction of interstellar travel by the Spacing Guild all make the traditional sci-fi battle tactics of starships in combat or aerial bombardment impossible. Instead, warfare has become once more about individuals facing one another, relying on their own ingenuity and training rather than advanced weaponry and technological prowess.

This makes the battle scenes in *Dune* much more intimate and emotionally resonant. If Duncan Idaho had been shot by a Harkonnen sniper, if Paul and Jamis's duel had been carried out with laser pistols, the impact would have been infinitely lessened. Here, we see how the restrictions placed on technology in the Imperium have had ripple effects that filter down to every single corner of the *Dune* universe.

TOP: 'I will kill him!' Feyd-Rautha (Sting) battles Muad'dib (Kyle MacLachlan) in 1984's *Dune*

BOTTOM LEFT: An engraving depicting two Roman gladiators in combat

BOTTOM RIGHT: Hi-ya! Bruce Lee karate-kicks a masked villain in TV's *The Green Hornet*, 1966–67

NEXT PAGE: 'Long live the fighters!' Duncan Idaho (Jason Momoa) takes on the Sardaukar in 2021's *Dune*

Chapter Seven: House Harkonnen

PITER DE VRIES AND THE MENTATS

Human 'computers' hard at work
at NASA's Langley Research
Center, Virginia, 1947

Of all the lessons contained in the Orange Catholic Bible, one has a greater impact on the universe of *Dune* than any other: 'Thou shalt not make a machine in the likeness of a human mind.' This blanket ban on 'thinking machines' is one of the few laws in the Landsraad that is never broken, even by monsters like the Harkonnen or rebels such as Muad'dib and the Fremen.

The law against the creation of artificial intelligence came into force following the Butlerian Jihad, a century-long anti-technological crusade that was fought some 10,000 years before the events recounted in *Dune*. Also known as the Great Revolt, the war would result in the destruction of every thinking machine on every known planet in the galaxy. Frank Herbert never made explicit the source of the name Butlerian Jihad, but it can be confidently supposed that it derives from the British novelist, critic and thinker Samuel Butler, whose utopian satire *Erewhon*, published in 1872, depicts a fictional land where machines have been outlawed.[2]

Inspired by the recent publication of Charles Darwin's *On the Origin of Species*, Butler penned an 1863 paper entitled 'Darwin among the Machines', putting forward the proposition that machines might undergo a process of natural selection equivalent to that of animal and plant life, and in the process acquire sentience and ultimately supplant their creators. 'In the course of ages we shall find ourselves the inferior race,' Butler wrote. 'That the time will come when the machines will hold the real supremacy over the world and its inhabitants is what no person of a truly philosophic mind can for a moment question.'[3]

Butler's ideas were so far ahead of their time that his contemporaries assumed he was joking or even satirizing Darwin. 'Nothing could be further from my intention,' he responded in the preface to his second edition of *Erewhon*, 'and few things would be more distasteful to me than any attempt to laugh at Mr Darwin.'[4] Instead, Butler went so far as to propose a war against machinery, a Luddite uprising to destroy the machines before they could become smart enough to enslave us. 'War to the death should be instantly proclaimed against them,' he urged. 'Every machine of every sort should be destroyed by the well-wisher of his species . . . let us at once go back to the primeval condition of the race.'[5]

Though far from a Luddite himself, Frank Herbert also had a practical distrust of technology, particularly computers, and the effect their increasing prevalence might have on humanity. He even made some uncanny, Butler-like predictions about the nature of these effects. In a 1968 piece for the *San Francisco Examiner* entitled '2068 AD', imagining life as it might be 100 years in the future, Herbert wrote: 'Computer stored data . . . had been used to harass and persecute those whose views didn't conform with those of the majority.'[6] Anyone who has borne witness to online shaming would recognize the wisdom of this prediction.

For Herbert, the most worrying thing about the rise of computers would be if they led people to begin thinking like computers themselves: 'One of the best things to come out of the home computer revolution,' he wrote, 'could be the general and widespread understanding of how severely limited logic really is.'[7] For Herbert, relying on computers to do our thinking removes the potential for intuition, for individual leaps of inspiration, that makes humanity so unique and unpredictable.

But perhaps the most remarkable thing is the source of the previous quote. It's from a book entitled *Without Me You're Nothing: The Essential Guide to Home Computers*, written by Frank Herbert with fellow author Max Barnard. Published in 1981, the book offers a potted history of home computing, a guide to using simple computer languages such as BASIC and a fair amount of philosophical musing on the status of computers in everyday life and how that might affect humanity in the future.

The title gives a not-so-subtle hint as to Herbert's feelings on the matter: throughout the book, he stresses the fact that computers are incapable of independent thought and are only as clever as the person operating them. He urges readers to be cautious and

'Technology is both a tool for helping humans and for destroying them'

FRANK HERBERT[8]

'Once men turned their thinking over to machines in the hopes that this would set them free. But that only permitted other men with machines to enslave them.'

REVEREND MOTHER GAIUS HELEN MOHIAM, *DUNE*[9]

Part Three: Giedi Prime

LEFT: The stains of
sapho: Mentat Thufir
Hawat (Freddie Jones)
in the 1984 film of *Dune*

ABOVE: Staff at NASA's
Supersonic Pressure
Tunnel in 1956, with the
'computers' in the front
row (left); 'Computer'
Mary W. Jackson would
go on to become NASA's
first black female
engineer (right)

selective about the technologies they employ and how they use them. He even coined his own word to describe this idea, 'technopeasantry', which he defined as: 'drawing support from technology, but doing so imaginatively . . . A peasant knows, you see, when and why to grab a shovel or a hoe. In the same way, we have to think out our own . . . technological options, and make decisions consciously.'[10] Still, the simple fact that a man who so distrusted computers would also author a guide to using them says a lot about Frank Herbert's nature: his willingness to explore subjects that he found off-putting or challenging, and his bone-dry sense of humour.

Removing artificial intelligence from his futuristic universe presented Frank Herbert with a fascinating set of challenges. How would complex mathematical problems be solved? How would trades and acquisitions be calculated, how would science continue to progress? How would the vast populations of thousands of worlds be accounted for?

Enter the mentats, or human computers. Trained from an early age to enhance their innate mental acuity through a process of strict practice and conditioning, mentats – like the Baron's twisted advisor, Piter De Vries, and the Atreides' trusted Master of Assassins, Thufir Hawat – further boost their cognitive abilities via the consumption of sapho juice, a natural extract that stains their lips a characteristic 'cranberry-coloured' shade. But though they are able to process vast and complex calculations, mentats are not purely logical – they also possess the human capabilities of intuition and emotion, allowing for leaps of perception that would be impossible for a simple computer. Also employed as military and political strategists, the mentats have developed their own ability to predict the future, given the correct information to work from. These predictions, however, can be imprecise.

The source of the mentats is easy to place. For the majority of Frank Herbert's lifetime, the word 'computer' was commonly applied not only to a machine, but to a human being employed to carry out calculations. Among the most notable were the women employed by the Jet Propulsion Laboratory in California and later by NASA in Houston, whose ability to carry out vast reams of complex computations would prove vital to both the war effort and the space programme. Women such as Barbara Cartwright, Mary W. Jackson, Katherine Johnson and Dorothy Vaughan – among many others – may have worked entirely behind the scenes, but their contribution to Allied victory in the Second World War and the success of the US Apollo programme is, ironically, incalculable.[11]

'He sensed it, the race consciousness that he could not escape'

FRANK HERBERT, DUNE [12]

That Frank Herbert knew of the existence of these specific women is unlikely; they were hardly household names. But he would certainly have known of the existence of 'human computers' and may even have had one within his own family. In *Dreamer of Dune*, Brian Herbert writes of his father's close relationship with his maternal grandmother, Mary Ellen Herbert, a committed quilt-maker with 'an incredible memory', who 'recalled details perfectly from decades before'. Though unable to read, she 'was a genius with figures . . . no matter how big the numbers'.[13]

This kind of innate intellectual ability must have made a powerful impression on young Frank, but it's not the only influence on his creation of the mentats. Scientific understanding of the human mind may have been in its relative infancy when *Dune* was written, but popular tales of people with extraordinary powers of recollection were common, from the fictional Sherlock Holmes and Mr Memory in Alfred Hitchcock's *The 39 Steps*, to real-life savants such as Solomon Shereshevsky, the Soviet-born 'mnemonist' with the ability to recall entire speeches word-for-word after a single hearing. Terms like 'photographic memory' and 'perfect recall' would have been familiar to Herbert, as would ideas of 'brain training' and memory improvement that go all the way back to the fourth century BC and the time of Aristotle, who wrote a treatise on memory and believed it could be improved by regular mental practice.

Another work of fiction that might well have influenced Herbert is *Flowers for Algernon* by Daniel Keyes, a short story published in 1959 and later expanded into a successful novel. The tale of a man with a severe learning disability who takes part in an experimental study intended to increase his intelligence, the story was first published in *The Magazine of Fantasy & Science Fiction* and would go on to win the 1960 Hugo Award for Best Short Story. Given that Frank Herbert was at the same time busily writing and submitting sci-fi stories for publication, it seems unlikely that he would have overlooked the winner of the form's most prestigious prize.

Oscar winner Cliff Robertson with Lilia Skala in 1968's Charly, based on the novel Flowers for Algernon

The mentats aren't the only beings in *Dune* to possess superhuman powers of memory. By consuming the most powerful form of the spice melange – 'the liquid exhalation of a dying sandworm'[14], known as the Water of Life – members of the Bene Gesserit Sisterhood are able to tap into another form of recall: genetic memory. In the trance that follows, Reverend Mothers can explore the memories of their mothers and grandmothers, all the way down the female line, through millennia of human history. They can even speak with the 'ghosts' of those ancestors and learn from their experience.

Here, Herbert was drawing on ideas of the 'collective unconscious', as espoused by the Swiss psychiatrist Carl Gustav Jung, another thinker whose influence on *Dune* can't be understated.[15] Born in 1875, Jung would, along with his close friend and colleague Sigmund Freud, become one of the founders of modern psychology. But where Freud's ideas tended to be rooted in earthly matters – sex, childhood, personal trauma – Jung's theories could be somewhat more outlandish, none more so than his belief in the collective unconscious.

Jung first defined the concept in his 1916 essay 'The Structure of the Unconscious', where he claimed: 'in dreams, fantasies, and other exceptional states of mind the most far-fetched mythological motifs and symbols can appear autochthonously (that is, without prompting) . . . These "primordial images" or "archetypes" . . . belong to the basic stock of the unconscious psyche and cannot be explained as personal acquisitions.'[16]

Among these archetypes, Jung identified a number of symbolic figures and images: the 'great mother', the 'wise old man', the tower, the shadow, the tree of life. He believed that such archetypes were not implanted in the human mind through experience, but were inherent in our unconscious from birth, handed down to us from previous generations. Here he again set himself apart from Freud and his belief that the unconscious at birth was *tabula rasa* – a blank slate.

Jung gathered evidence to support his claim, drawing on the testimonies of his psychiatric patients: 'The snake-motif was certainly not an individual acquisition of

the dreamer,' he wrote, 'for snake-dreams are very common even among city-dwellers who have probably never seen a real snake.'[17] In later writings he also explored ideas of instinct, how certain animals are able to carry out surprisingly complex tasks without having been 'taught' to do so. He identified five inherent human instincts: hunger, sexuality, activity, reflection and creativity.[18]

Here, Jung's ideas begin to overlap with another theory that was being explored in the late nineteenth and early twentieth centuries: genetic memory. Like the theory of collective unconscious, genetic memory posits that memories can be passed down from parent to child – only here they exist not in some globe-spanning shared subconscious but encoded within our individual genes. The German evolutionary biologist Richard Wolfgang Semon was one of its most committed proponents, coining the term 'engram' to describe the physical source of memories within the brain.[19] However, his efforts to locate one proved fruitless.

Over the past century, ideas of genetic memory have largely been discredited (though fascinatingly, studies involving mice have shown that fear-responses to certain smells can be passed down from one generation to the next). But in fiction, genetic memory remains a popular theme, from Jack London's 1907 novel *Before Adam*, about a modern man who dreams the life of a prehistoric hominid, to a pair of novels published not long before *Dune*: Arthur C. Clarke's *Childhood's End*, in which it is revealed that human 'race memories' of the Devil have been inspired by early encounters with an alien race, to Pierre Boule's original 1963 book *Planet of the Apes*, in which a hypnotized human recalls via genetic memory the events that led to the downfall of our species and its replacement by intelligent apes.

But Frank Herbert's exploration of the subject remains perhaps the most thorough and intriguing – and in his customary manner, he depicts both sides of the coin. While in *Dune* the power of genetic memory is treated as a great gift, a way to connect each generation with the thousands that came before it, in later books the practice becomes increasingly troublesome, leading in *Children of Dune* to the subjugation of existing personalities by 'ghosts' from the past, and allowing for the disembodied reincarnation of the series' most dastardly villain.

CHAPTER NINE
THE CHOAM CORPORATION

Burning oil wells in the
aftermath of Operation
Desert Storm, Kuwait, 1991

For Baron Vladimir Harkonnen, the ultimate prize
for all his scheming would be, as he tells his nephew
Feyd-Rautha, 'an irrevocable directorship in the
CHOAM company', with the promise of wealth
beyond the boy's 'wildest imaginings'. So what is
CHOAM, and why is its membership so highly prized?

Under its full title *Combine Honnete Ober Advancer Mercantiles* – a name derived from several languages, notably French, and roughly translated as Honorable Union for the Advancement of Greater Trade – CHOAM is the publicly owned corporation that controls the movement of all goods within the Imperium: 'logs, donkeys, horses, cows, lumber, dung, sharks, whale fur – the most prosaic and the most exotic.'[2] While shares in the Corporation are distributed throughout the Great Houses and Houses Minor that make up the governing body known as the Landsraad, the largest stakeholder is the Padishah Emperor, giving him control over CHOAM and thereby over the other Houses. The Spacing Guild and the Bene Gesserit also control shares in CHOAM, but they act as silent partners, working behind the scenes.

Like any modern corporation, CHOAM has a board of directors, drawn from the most powerful Great Houses and given the task of steering the Corporation's fortunes. Given great social status, these directors are also notoriously corrupt, using their position to dip into the CHOAM coffers and siphon off as much wealth as they can. This, then, is the prize the Baron seeks: the chance not just to gain enormous power, but to become fabulously wealthy into the bargain.

For Frank Herbert, CHOAM was the key to another of his ambitions with *Dune*: 'to penetrate the interlocked workings of politics and economics.'[3] The Corporation would be directly inspired by a real-world entity that was, at the time of the book's creation, a brand-new force in the world: OPEC, or the Organization of the Petroleum Exporting Countries.

Formed in 1960 by five oil-rich nations – Iran, Iraq, Kuwait, Saudi Arabia and Venezuela – OPEC's founding aim was to reduce the involvement of outside nations, such as Britain and America, in the production and exporting of oil, and retain as much of the profits for themselves as possible. Efforts to take such action unilaterally had, in the past, proved troublesome – Iran's efforts to nationalize their oil industry in 1953 led to a coup sponsored by the UK and US – so it was decided that safety in numbers might be the best approach.

But OPEC wasn't just about self-preservation. Under the direction of the OPEC Conference – its equivalent of a board of directors, headed by the OPEC Secretary General – the organization also allowed its members to control the price of oil by limiting world supply, resulting in greatly increased profits. Over the decades, however, those same members have been accused of ignoring the organization's agreed-upon limits and producing as much oil as possible.[4]

OPEC has always been to some extent unstable, thanks to the vast economic, religious and cultural differences between its member nations. While it may be committed to finding non-military solutions to conflicts over the possession of oil and its sources, this has not always been possible: during OPEC's lifetime the world has seen countless wars and upheavals at least partly influenced by the possession of oil, from the Yom Kippur War between Israel and a coalition of Arab states to the Gulf Wars precipitated by conflicts between OPEC members Iraq and Kuwait.

The resonances with *Dune* are inescapable. As previously noted, the spice melange can be viewed as a direct metaphor for oil – it enables transportation, it's found in a desert environment and it cannot be mined without great risk. Both substances are the most valued commodity in their respective time periods, and this very pricelessness leads to conflict between the powers who would possess them.

But while the struggle between the Harkonnens, the Atreides, the Imperium and the Fremen for control of Arrakis and its spice sands may ring true to modern audiences in the wake of two Gulf Wars and the occupation of Iraq, it's important to remember that

'The treasure hid in the sand': Delegates at an OPEC oil ministers meeting in 1976

'CHOAM is OPEC'

FRANK HERBERT,
'DUNE GENESIS'

'For they shall suck of the abundance of the seas, and the treasure hid in the sand'

DEUTERONOMY 33:19, QUOTED IN *DUNE*[5]

Frank Herbert was writing *before* any of this had occurred. He was simply looking at the upheavals then taking place in the Middle East, at the formation of OPEC and the historical wars for power in oil-rich regions, and letting his imagination fill in the rest.

This has led many readers to observe that, for a book so concerned with prescience and foresight, *Dune* is itself an eerily prophetic novel. Its prediction of colonial powers pillaging desert lands for profit has come true countless times, while the Fremen with their guerrilla tactics and indiscriminate attacks on the Harkonnens find obvious parallels in the armed insurgency that followed the US occupations of Iraq and Afghanistan. Indeed, the very notion of a vastly superior technological force losing a war to a ragtag indigenous army must have seemed, at the time of publication, like pure fiction; not so in the wake of the conflicts of Vietnam and Afghanistan.

Of course, historians can always counter claims that Frank Herbert was some kind of prophet by pointing out that such things had been going on for centuries – see, for example, the Arab Revolt of 1917. Or, as Herbert himself put it in an essay entitled 'Science Fiction and a World in Crisis': 'Every now and then we (sci-fi writers) hit paydirt. Realpolitik catches up with fiction.'[6]

But while CHOAM may be OPEC, it isn't *only* OPEC. Another key inspiration behind this all-powerful mercantile corporation was an organization that came and went centuries before Frank Herbert's birth – the Dutch East India Company.

Formed in 1602 to capitalize on the vast profits being made on the importation to Europe of spices from the Far East, the company – officially known as *Vereenigde Oostindische Compagnie* (United East India Company) or the VOC – would become by far the most successful economic entity of its time, employing more people, owning more ships and making greater profits than the rest of the European spice trade combined.

Like CHOAM, the VOC was a mercantile organization, founded on trade between organizations and nations (or planets). And like CHOAM, the VOC's wealth came

from the importation of spices, among them nutmeg, saffron, pepper, cardamom and cinnamon. Many of these weren't merely prized as flavourings, but as status symbols or markers of wealth[7] and also for their medicinal and/or mind-expanding properties: saffron was used as a pain reliever, while nutmeg was smoked for its subtle hallucinogenic properties.

But the VOC was much more than just a company, in the sense that modern readers might understand it. In many ways it was closer to a nation, with a 'capital city' at Jakarta in Indonesia, enough ships and soldiers to wage wars for control of resources, and the right under Dutch law to imprison and execute criminals, negotiate treaties and print its own currency.

Still, the Dutch East India company was run according to corporate rules, with managing directors and shareholders at the top, followed by layers of managers, merchants, traders, sailors and soldiers, and at the bottom a vast number of unskilled labourers and plantation workers largely drawn from the local populace, many of whom were simply slave labour.[8] Indeed, the VOC was one of the driving forces behind the Dutch slave trade, leading to the deaths of countless thousands of Eurasian and African people. It could also be a brutal conquering force: when in 1609 the population of the Banda Islands in Indonesia attempted to resist VOC control of their nutmeg plantations, the company's reprisals resulted in the deaths of the vast majority of the population, whether by violence or disease, while the survivors were enslaved and put to work on their own land.[9]

In the Imperium of *Dune* we learn that slavery is still practised: the Emperor possesses slave-concubines, while the Baron Harkonnen indulges his sexual desires with bought slaves and Feyd-Rautha uses indentured fighters to hone his fighting skills. Though it is never spelled out, we must assume that the trade in such slaves is overseen – like all commerce in this universe – by CHOAM.

The Dutch East India company was ultimately undone by several factors: increased resistance from local forces; the growth of cheaper commodities, such as sugar, from Brazil; and its involvement in the Fourth Anglo-Dutch War, which led to the diminution of the Dutch Empire and the growth of the British. But as with CHOAM, the VOC was also being eaten up from within, as its directors and managers siphoned off profits for themselves – and reasonably so, given that the company was a notoriously poor payer whose employees had the worrying tendency to die on the job.

Whether the corruption of its directors would have ultimately ended CHOAM is unknown – before that can happen, the company is undermined by the God Emperor Leto II, who severely restricts its activities during his 3,500 year reign. However, given Frank Herbert's frequently expressed belief that all large organizations are ultimately undone by their own hubris, we can probably assume that it would. In this, CHOAM resembles another great power in the universe – the greatest of all, in fact.

TOP: A 1681 plan of Batavia, capital of the Dutch East Indies and now the site of Jakarta, Indonesia

BOTTOM LEFT: A 1783 illustration depicting a VOC soldier in uniform

BOTtOM RIGHT: This 1708 illustration shows inhabitants of the historical region of Arakan selling slaves to the Dutch East India Company

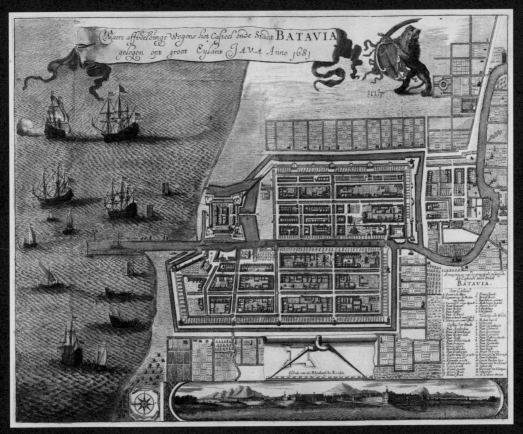

PART FOUR

KORHDHZ

HOUSE CORRINO AND THE PADISHAH EMPEROR

Absolute power: a 1579
portrait of the Ottoman
Sultan, Murad I

Frank Herbert distrusted leaders. Indeed, all government was, to him, inherently undependable and destined to betray the people it was meant to serve. He may not have been a card-carrying political party member; he may even have questioned the entire nature of democracy. But he was, in his own words, 'a political animal' who had once 'had two offices in Washington DC . . . I've been on the inside of the apple, so I know what's going on back there'.[1]

'All governments suffer a recurring problem: power attracts pathological personalities. It is not that power corrupts, but that power is a magnet to the corruptible.'

FRANK HERBERT, CHAPTERHOUSE: DUNE [2]

And *Dune* is undoubtedly a political work, though never a straightforward one. As we've seen, ideologues on all sides of the political spectrum have tried to claim the book as their own, from fascists who appreciate its messianic fervour and concern with eugenics, to progressives who cite its empathy with First Nations peoples and its anti-imperialist stance. But *Dune* continues to resist easy categorization, in large part because its author's political beliefs were, as Daniel Immerwahr writes, 'all over the map',[3] leaning often to the right – he supported Ronald Reagan for president – but sometimes the other way, as with his ecological activism, stated belief in drug legalization[4] and outspoken opposition to the Vietnam War.

One thing remained consistent, however: like his former employers in the Republican Party, Frank Herbert had a lifelong desire to see government reduced. As he told the ecological magazine *Mother Earth News* as part of its playfully titled Plowboy Interview series in 1981: 'There is definitely an implicit warning in a lot of my work against big government . . . I think it's vital that men and women learn to mistrust all forms of powerful, centralized authority.'[5] Nowhere does this anti-authoritarian tendency come into sharper relief than in the person of *Dune*'s all-powerful sovereign, the 81st Padishah Emperor, Shaddam IV.

The head of House Corrino, whose sons have ruled the Imperium for some 10,000 years, Shaddam resides on the planet Kaitain – a world kept hidden in Frank Herbert's books, though we can infer that it is a wealthy, opulent place. Though they may once have been great warriors, reigning triumphant at the Battle of Corrin, the members of House Corrino have gradually slid into decay, becoming less and less connected to their subjects and losing themselves in the trappings of wealth and privilege – what Herbert describes in his appendices as, 'Court functions and the pomp of office'.[6] In the process, the Imperium has left itself open to attack from within – which of course arrives in the form of Paul Atreides and his Fremen.

'The pomp of office':
Padishah Emperor Shaddam IV
(Jose Ferrer) in 1984's *Dune*

'You cannot understand history unless you understand its flowings, its currents and the way leaders move within such forces'

LETO II, *GOD EMPEROR OF DUNE* [1]

For Herbert, the trappings of power inevitably lead to corruption. In *Dune*, Duke Leto bemoans 'the melancholy degeneration of the Great Houses,'[8] while in interviews the author would claim: 'great power centers such as the Kremlin, the Pentagon, Quai d'Orsay, Sandhurst become essentially cesspools really, because they get so many people there who want power for the sake of power, and it's my estimation of it that a high percentage of these people are certifiable.'[9] This idea that those who desire power are unhinged was a favourite theme: 'It is the systems themselves that I see as dangerous,' he wrote in 'Dune Genesis'. 'Power structures tend to attract people who want power for the sake of power, and . . . a significant proportion of such people are imbalanced – in a word, insane.'[10]

What we learn of the Emperor before his exile and death places him alongside the most extravagant of history's leaders: he sits on a vast throne, 'a massive chair carved from a single piece of Hagal quartz',[11] and dresses in military garb to match the uniforms of his royal guard, the Sardaukar. He speaks softly until roused, and his final response to the Arrakis revolt is a threat to 'purge this planet'[12] of every living soul. The name Shaddam is clearly Arabic in origin and offers one more eerie precursor of the Gulf War, and another all-powerful and evidently 'imbalanced' leader who dwelt in grotesque opulence until his reign was abruptly and ignominiously brought to an end.

Of course, this is another coincidence – Saddam Hussein wouldn't rule Iraq until 1979, long after *Dune*'s publication. In fact, the Arabic roots of the Emperor's name may be a sideways reference to another of Frank Herbert's influences, a man whose ideas run throughout *Dune* and its sequels: the fourteenth-century thinker, historian and father of sociology, Ibn Khaldun.

In *Dune*, the Fremen of the desert carry and quote from a combined survival handbook and religious manual known as the *Kitab al-Ibar* or *Book of Lessons*. The same title was given by the Tunisian-born polymath Ibn Khaldun to his vast seven-volume historical study, a sprawling work that not only encompassed the entire history of civilization up to that point, but also included a book-length introduction, the *Muqaddimah*, that laid much of the groundwork for what would become known as sociology. Indeed, the *Muqaddimah* remains politically influential to the present day, particularly among Frank Herbert's fellow small-government advocates. None other than Republican President Ronald Reagan directly cited Ibn Khaldun – with his belief in stratified societies and his rejection of governmental bureaucracy – as an influence on his 'Reaganomic' policies.[13]

Born in Tunis in 1332 under the full name of Abdurahman bin Muhammad bin Muhammad bin Muhammad bin Al-Hasan bin Jabir bin Muhammad bin Ibrahim bin Abdurahman bin Ibn Khaldun al-Hadrami, Ibn Khaldun was the son of a wealthy Muslim family who could claim direct descent from a companion of the Prophet Mohammed. After losing both his parents to the plague, the Black Death, and following a spell in prison for acting against an employer's wishes, Ibn Khaldun would make the move into politics, carrying out diplomatic duties for numerous North African viziers and sultans, including a mission to the Spanish court of Pedro the Cruel. At the same time, he would develop strong ties to the Berber tribes of the Northern Sahara, under whose protection he would write his *Muqaddimah*.

In the book, Khaldun espouses a cyclical theory of history by looking at the rise and fall of empires, how they come about and why they inevitably collapse.[14] For him, humanity could be divided into two essential groups: sedentary peoples, who tended to grow crops and congregate in towns and ultimately cities; and nomads, who survived by raising animals, necessitating a constant movement from one place to another in search of fresh grazing. While the peoples of town and city would be better educated and more comfortable, this luxury would inevitably cause them to grow idle and complacent. Meanwhile, the nomads would only become tougher, hardened by their environment and united by religious belief, seasoning them into warriors who would eventually set their sights on the cities, conquering and capturing them for themselves. At which point the cycle would start again: having acquired the wealth of the cities the nomads would themselves become sedentary, take on the cultural interests of their predecessors and in their turn grow corrupt and idle.

The relevance of these ideas to *Dune* is impossible to miss.[15] The Fremen are, of course, nomadic, devout, fierce and nimble; their enemies, the Harkonnen and the Padishah Emperor, are corrupt, complacent and resistant to change. War is inevitable, as is Fremen victory. As Muad'dib admits when recalling his upbringing on Caladan: 'The price we paid was the price men have always paid for achieving a paradise in this life – we went soft, we lost our edge.'[16] It is only in the harsh environment of the desert, under the guidance of the Fremen, that Paul can regain this aggressive 'edge'.

In Herbert's sequels, however, the wheel turns again. In *Dune Messiah* it is the Fremen who lose their way; the court of Muad'dib overflows with petty bureaucrats and corrupt, conniving schemers and the inevitable rot sets in. It's up to Paul's son, Leto II, to learn the lessons of Ibn Khaldun, to find a way to break the cycle of violence, degeneration and decay.

The iron fist within the velvet glove of imperial authority is of course the Sardaukar, that seemingly inexhaustible force of indomitable warriors who can be unleashed upon any House that dares to stand against the throne. Described as 'soldier-fanatics', the Sardaukar are by far the most feared and formidable military unit in the Imperium, at least until the rise of the Fremen.

In fact, many of Frank Herbert's influences when creating the Fremen might also apply to the Sardaukar. Both are trained from birth to be warriors, with the weak weeded out in the manner of ancient Sparta. Both are products of the Ibn Khaldun school of hard knocks, forced to survive in relentless, inhospitable environments: for the Sardaukar this is the Emperor's prison planet of Salusa Secundus, once the home of House Corrino until it was laid waste. And both are bonded by a powerful religious feeling: in the case of the Sardaukar, this centres upon the person of the Emperor and the gifts he bestows – as Thufir Hawat says in *Dune*: 'Rich living, beautiful women, fine mansions . . . The commonest Sardaukar trooper lives a life, in many respects, as exalted as that of any member of a Great House.'[17]

But there are two additional influences on the Sardaukar, two legendary fighting forces from history whose names struck fear into those who opposed them. The first is the Praetorian Guard, the core faction of the Roman Army established by Augustus in 27 BC, who for three centuries served as bodyguards to the emperor. Unlike the Sardaukar, the Praetorians were not trained from birth; instead, they were hand-picked from the ranks of the Roman Army, often veterans of foreign campaigns who had distinguished themselves in battle. Indeed, their military service tended to be shorter than that of the regular conscripted soldier: 12 years as opposed to 16. But they received generous rewards from their patron: their pay was far more generous than the regular army wage and they often received gifts and bonuses, particularly on feast days.

Like the Sardaukar, the Praetorians were not merely bodyguards and soldiers working to enforce the emperor's will. They also served as his intelligence-gathering service, spying on the emperor's enemies, uncovering plots against his person and rounding up those who spoke against him. The Sardaukar's role as undercover agents for the Emperor is made clear in *Dune*'s sequels: in *Dune Messiah*, Chani weeds out a pair of Sardaukar spies on a mission to infiltrate the court of Muad'dib, while in *Children of Dune* the Emperor's eldest daughter, Princess Wensicia, uses the last remaining Sardaukar warriors to carry out an elaborate assassination plot against Paul's young children, training ferocious laza tigers to hunt down and attack the twins Ghanima and Leto.

But in one notable aspect the Sardaukar and the Praetorian Guard differ dramatically. The idea of a Sardaukar soldier turning against his Emperor is unthinkable – absolute loyalty is drilled into them from birth and bought time and again with rewards and graces. The Praetorian Guard were not so reliable. Despite having no formal political power, they nonetheless played a key role in choosing the next emperor, using their fearsome military heft to 'influence' those senators charged with deciding the imperial succession. And despite being officially charged with uncovering plots against the emperor, the Praetorians actually took part in several. They conspired with senators to murder Emperor Caligula and place his uncle Claudius on the throne, then in AD 193 they even went so far as to sell the empire, assassinating the sitting emperor, Pertinax, and installing his successor, Didius Julianus, all for a generous fee. Sadly for Didius and his Praetorian backers, he only ruled for nine weeks before civil war broke out and he lost his throne to Septimius Severus, who routed the Praetorians and replaced them with his own men.[18]

Why did the Praetorian Guard revolt when the Sardaukar do not? The answer may lie in the other major influence that Frank Herbert drew on when creating this race of fanatical warriors.

For centuries, the most feared fighting force in Europe were the Janissaries, an elite infantry unit bound to the Sultan of the Ottoman Empire. From the sack of Constantinople in 1453, through countless wars against a multiplicity of foes, to their eventual disbandment in the nineteenth century, the Janissary corps were the very cornerstone of Ottoman power.

It was the fourteenth-century sultan, Murad I, who first placed a levy on all slaves taken in battle, claiming one-fifth for himself, and it was from this pool of human labour that the first Janissaries were trained. Later they would be taken from the ranks of child slaves under a system known as *devşirme,* whereby boys of non-Muslim extraction, usually Albanians, Bulgarians and Bosnians between the ages of six and 14, would be taken from their families, converted to Islam and then ruthlessly trained in the military arts. Kept in isolated barracks and taught to treat the Janissary corps as their home and the Sultan as their father, these boys would grow into fiercely loyal men.

It helped that – as with the Praetorians and the Sardaukar – once the training period was over, the Janissaries were far better treated than many of their fellow subjects. In Ottoman society it wasn't unusual for slaves to claim a higher social standing than their supposedly 'free' contemporaries, so not only were these enslaved soldiers paid a regular wage and granted a generous portion of the spoils from any conquest, they were also highly respected, becoming a kind of military aristocracy. Though forbidden to marry or practise a trade until their term of service ended at age 40, many would go on to prosper in later life. Indeed, by the sixteenth century it wasn't uncommon for parents to bribe the Turkish authorities to take their sons, knowing they'd have a greater chance as a slave soldier than if they remained at home.[19]

The Janissaries were also better equipped for battle than their fellow soldiers. Originally trained in archery and the use of a short sword known as a *yatagan*, when the use of muskets became widespread in the fifteenth century the Janissaries were soon experts in their battlefield deployment. They had their own support corps to set up their camps and cook their food, as well as trained medical professionals and even their own travelling musicians.

But despite their enforced bonding, religious inculcation and generous treatment, over the centuries the Janissaries became, like the Praetorian Guard, simply too powerful to control. By the seventeenth century, the corps was so large that its leaders could influence political policy, and even overthrow the sultan himself. Having first abandoned the law against marriage, in 1648 they abolished slave recruitment and instead began to hand-pick their own members, often the sons of serving officers. This in turn led to an inevitable softening of the training process: though still rigorous, it wasn't nearly as harsh and single-minded as the brutal discipline undergone by their forebears.

Following a number of Janissary-led coups and revolts, it was Sultan Mahmud II who, in the guise of a truce with the corps, was finally able to secure enough personal power and military backing to have them forcefully disbanded. The resulting mutiny – which would become known as the 'Auspicious Incident' – led to Janissary forces marching on the Sultan's palace, where the majority of them were cut down by artillery fire while the rest were exiled or executed.[20]

Again, we see parallels with the Sardaukar, of whom Herbert writes in his glossary, 'by the time of Shaddam IV, while they were still formidable, their strength had been sapped by overconfidence'.[21] But they are nonetheless feared enough to act as the supreme military power in the universe, holding in check that power-hungry conglomeration of warring elites, noble Houses and private armies that comprise the Imperium's largest governing body.

This section of an illuminated manuscript shows Janissary recruitment in the Ottoman Empire, c. 1558

CHAPTER ELEVEN

THE LANDSRAAD

The Sardaukar may be the most direct tool of oppression in the *Dune* universe, but they are by no means the only one. Almost as powerful is simple tradition, and a political system so rigid and so ancient that no one even thinks to question it. The class structure of the Imperium is strictly feudal, organized according to an ancient system known as *faufreluches*, with its guiding motto: 'A place for every man and every man in his place.'[1]

'If patterns teach me anything it's that patterns are repeated'

LETO II, *GOD EMPEROR OF DUNE*[2]

The term itself is a take on a French word, fanfreluches, meaning trimming or decoration, and again it's borrowed from Lesley Blanch and The Sabres of Paradise (see page 40), where it refers to the tassels found on the saddles of Russian cavalry horses: a symbol of imperial pomp and trumpery.

At the top of the feudal pyramid sits the Padishah Emperor, the male heir to House Corrino and a man with vast influence and near-infinite resources. But the Emperor's power is not limitless, for he must still work alongside the Landsraad, a political body representing the Great Houses and the Houses Minor, and a jostling, unruly collection of competing interests. The idea is that the Landsraad and the Emperor serve to balance one another out, the one great power held in check by thousands of lesser powers all working together. And indeed, for 10 millennia the system has worked largely as it was supposed to, delivering political stability, relative peace and a time of plenty – at least, for those at the top.

Derived from German and literally meaning 'council of the land', the word *Landsraad* was in common usage until relatively recently. For the Danes, *landsråd* was, until 1950, the name given to a pair of provincial bodies – one north, one south – overseeing the governance of colonial Greenland,[3] until they were replaced by the Greenland Home Rule Government. This might have been from where Herbert took his inspiration: 'Landsraad is an old Scandinavian word for an assembly of landowners,' he would tell *Vertex* magazine in 1973. 'It's historically accurate in that it was an assembly . . . it's the landed gentry.'[4] By the time of *Dune*, the gentry have become somewhat more than 'landed': in Herbert's glossary he defines a House as the 'ruling Clan of a planet or planetary system'[5] with interests spanning several worlds, while the Houses Minor are generally restricted to a single planet.

But despite their enormous, galaxy-spanning power, the Houses of the Landsraad still closely resemble their Earthly forebears: the feudal powers of medieval Europe. Derived from the Latin word *feodum*, meaning fief, the term *feudalism* is actually a retrospective one, applied by historians to a system of class-based rule common

A group shot of the North Greenlandic Landsraad in 1939 by photographer Jette Bang

Non est potestas Super Terram quæ Comparetur ei. Iob. 41. 24.

LEVIATHAN

Or

THE MATTER, FORME
and POWER of A COMMON-
WEALTH ECCLESIASTICALL
and CIVIL.

By THOMAS HOBBES
of MALMESBVRY.

London
Printed for Andrew Crooke
1651.

across Europe and the Holy Roman Empire from approximately the ninth to the fifteenth centuries. Feudalism divided people into rigid social strata according to birth, wealth, religious factors and the ownership of land.[6] The term hasn't only been applied to Europe – feudal societies can historically be found in China, India, America at the time of slavery and, of course, Japan, whose culture, as we've seen, was an influence on Herbert. But given his use of Danish and French-derived terms alongside European words like fief, clan and convention, it seems reasonable that we keep our focus there.

Emerging from the Roman system of slave-based patronage, the concept of feudalism was, at the root, one of mutual support: the vassal or subject would provide services to his lord, from the provision of food and saleable goods to the staffing of his household, and in return the lord would guarantee protection and a place on his land. Organized into a series of fiefs – areas of property and specific rights granted to the lord by a king or emperor – the system was intended to encourage loyalty and establish fairness on all levels. Laws were instituted to enshrine the rights of peasants as well as lords, who were forbidden from striking or otherwise abusing their workforce unless mandated to do so by a judge. These noble intentions are embodied by Herbert in the form of House Atreides and its reasonable, fair-minded Duke, who rules Caladan through mutual respect and understanding with his subjects.

In reality, of course, feudalism wasn't so agreeable. Like their fictional descendants, the Padishah Emperor and House Harkonnen, the European aristocratic class were often corrupt, venal and lazy, surrounding themselves with luxuries while their serfs worked in thankless poverty and ignorance. Peasant men could be called into military service at the merest whim of their liege lord, resulting in the deaths of thousands of untrained and ill-equipped soldiers. Religion was used as a weapon of control: backed by the church, the aristocracy could claim that their right to rule was granted by God, meaning that any peasant who questioned his or her place in society was going against the will of the Almighty. In a desperate, downtrodden, God-fearing society like medieval Europe, very few would dare.

Following the Black Death in the fourteenth century, which wiped out some 60 per cent of the continent's citizens, the hold of the feudal system was weakened across Europe; by the end of the following century the practice was largely at an end. It would persist in certain societies, clinging on in France until the Revolution in 1790, while the British-owned Channel Island of Sark was theoretically feudal until as late as 2008, owned by the billionaire Barclay brothers and ruled by an unelected *Seigneur*.

Of course, many would argue that the basic principles of feudalism – unbreachable social barriers, religious control, a small but powerful aristocracy ruling by threat and tradition over a large, hard-working underclass – still very much apply in many countries, and that this question of class-based inequality and exploitation is perhaps even more pressing now than when Frank Herbert was writing. But that's a conversation for another book.

As well as upholding the strict feudal traditions of *faufreluches*, the Landsraad is the only body in the galaxy with the power to oversee the formal process known as *kanly*, or vendetta, between two Houses. As we've seen, the use of atomic weaponry was outlawed following the Butlerian Jihad, with new rules of warfare codified according to the Great Convention, an agreement between the Great Houses, the Emperor and the Spacing Guild intended to ensure the protection of civilian life. The Convention also laid down the codes of *kanly*, a kind of ceremonial cold war that can be carried out via assassination, infiltration and closely regulated violence, and passed on from generation to generation until one side or the other is defeated.

The divine right of kings, as depicted in a 1651 engraving by Abraham Bosse used as the frontispiece of *Leviathan* by Thomas Hobbes

The word is derived from the Turkish language, where *kanli* means bloody, or blood enemy. But the practice of vendetta – an Italian term originating in the Latin word *vindicta*, meaning vengeance – goes back to the Ancient Greeks, where the right of a wronged party to seek reparation was viewed as entirely natural.[7] Indeed, the plot of the *Iliad* is essentially a series of vengeful acts: the Trojan war is sparked by the Greek desire for revenge following the abduction of Helen, and ends after Achilles kills Hector in revenge for the death of his companion Patroclus. These acts are aided and abetted by the gods, whose right of divine retribution is absolute.

Legally mandated vendettas would become commonplace in medieval Europe, where the German word *faida* was used to describe the formal practice of retribution following the death of a family member – it would later be corrupted into the English word feud. In Japan, *katakiuchi* or revenge killings were historically seen as an appropriate way for a samurai family or clan to maintain its honour. But blood feuds would become especially common in nineteenth-century rural Corsica – resulting, by some accounts, in the deaths of over 4,000 people during a 30-year period[8] – and in the US during the Wild West era: the storied rivalry between the wealthy Hatfield family of West Virginia and their less-well-off rivals, the McCoys of Kentucky, would lead to several murders and a Supreme Court trial.[9]

Again, the practice of vendetta is by no means a thing of the past. In Albania, traditions of blood feuding that have historically killed some 10,000 people show no signs of stopping,[10] while in Southern Italy the existence of powerful crime families mean that age-old feuds between individuals, clans and even entire villages – of the kind seen in gangster movies like *The Godfather Part II* and *Gomorrah* – still rage to this day. At least in *Dune* these feuds operate under strict, life-preserving conditions – in the real world they tend to be unlimited, bloody and ruthless.

BOTTOM LEFT: The Hatfield family, whose feud with the McCoy clan has passed into Wild West legend

BOTTOM RIGHT: An act of vengeance in feudal Japan, as depicted in *Revenge of the Soga Brothers* by Utagawa Hiroshige, 1843–47

RIGHT: Feuds and 'honour killings' form the bedrock of gangster films like *The Godfather Part II* (top) and *Gomorrah* (bottom)

CHAPTER TWELVE
THE SPACING
GUILD

The last but by no means the least of the great powers that steer the fortunes of *Dune*'s Galactic Imperium is the Spacing Guild, that enigmatic and highly secretive organization tasked with overseeing all interplanetary travel.

Like that other school of physical and mental discipline, the Bene Gesserit, the Guild of Navigators was formed in the wake of the Butlerian Jihad, its purpose to train humans to navigate ships at faster-than-light speeds without the use of computers. To achieve this, Guild navigators utilize the spice melange, which precipitates 'the "navigation trance", by which a translight pathway could be "seen" before it was travelled'[1] – allowing them to guide their vast heighliner ships safely through interstellar space. However, the spice also serves to mutate the navigators, leading them to appear, like Edric in Dune Messiah, 'vaguely humanoid, with finned feet and hugely fanned membranous hands'.[2]

The Guild's monopoly on interstellar haulage might suggest parallels with transportation unions such as the Teamsters, the notorious truckers' union founded in the US in 1903 and at the height of its headline-grabbing power under corrupt president Jimmy Hoffa just as Frank Herbert was writing Dune. But that organization is much too blue-collar and quotidian to be seen as an inspiration for the rarefied, elitist Spacing Guild. Instead, a closer equivalence might be drawn with that mysterious fraternal organization whose murky rituals and centuries-long influence have made it one of the most talked-about 'secret' societies in existence: the order of Freemasons.

The origins of Freemasonry are shrouded in myth, though the order is believed to have emerged from the stonemasons' guilds operating across medieval Europe. It wasn't until the eighteenth century, however, that its traditions became more established, leading to the creation of some of the first masonic 'lodges' (or at least the first to be publicly recognized). The year 1723 saw the publication of The Constitutions of the Free-Masons, a set of rules and practices that was widely distributed throughout lodges in the UK, the US and across Europe.[3] At the same time, lurid rumours of their supposed involvement in various centuries-old conspiracies began to spread, not least among the Masons themselves. Over the years their notoriety has continued to grow, thanks in part to the continued secrecy under which the society operates, but also to countless works of sensationalist fiction from the Sherlock Holmes novel The Sign of the Four[4] to Da Vinci Code author Dan Brown's gaudy conspiracy thriller The Lost Symbol.[5]

The parallels between the Spacing Guild and the popular perception of the Freemasons are several. Both operate in darkness, nursing their own secretive ambitions. Both offer an apolitical public face – the Masons are simply a society of craftsmen, while the Spacing Guild just fly ships – while at the same time meddling in affairs of state, from steering the course of a nation (no less than 14 US presidents were Freemasons, from George Washington to Gerald Ford) to providing the transport necessary to move legions of imperial troops to Arrakis to destroy the Atreides.

Of course, the reality of Freemasonry is much more mundane than the legends suggest: their traditions and ceremonies may be arcane, but the organization really does just exist to forge business relationships between its members (unless, of course, that's just what they want us to think). But whether or not the conspiracies swirling around the Freemasons are true is irrelevant: they are shrouded in mystery and, just like the Spacing Guild, that's exactly how they want it.

✳

With poetic names like Arrakis, Caladan and Richesse, one could easily assume that the planets visited by the Spacing Guild in Dune and its sequels are entirely imaginary. In fact, many of the worlds of Dune are based upon real locations within our own Milky Way Galaxy, chosen by Frank Herbert from his own researches into astronomy. Though our own planet, Earth, no longer exists – 'Our ancestral worlds have gone,' mourns the Bene Gesserit, Darwi Odrade, in Chapterhouse: Dune[6] – memories of it still live in the genetic recollections of the Sisterhood, in the tales of the Fremen and other ancient societies, and in the names of stars and planets, many of them drawn from our current astronomical catalogue.

A mutant Guild Navigator floats in a tank filled with spice gas, from 1984's Dune

'The singular multiplicity of this universe draws my deepest attention. It is a thing of ultimate beauty.'

LETO II, *GOD EMPEROR OF DUNE*[7]

ARRAKIS

CALADAN

GIEDI PRIME

KAITAIN

LEFT: Artist Lennart Dörr's
impressions of the worlds
of Dune – the rings around
Kaitain were first suggested
by the 1984 film

RIGHT: Spaceship designs by
the legendary Chris Foss
for the first, unsuccessful
attempt to bring Dune to the
screen: a damaged pirate ship
leaking spice (top) and a
spice container ship (bottom)

'And so, in silence, we walked the surface of a dying world'

EDGAR RICE BURROUGHS,
A PRINCESS OF MARS [8]

As detailed by Joseph M. Daniels in his exhaustively researched 1999 article 'The Stars and Planets of Frank Herbert's *Dune*: A Gazetteer',[9] the planet Arrakis is located some 89 light years from Earth in the multi-star system of Mu Draconis, near the 'head' of the constellation we know as Draco. Visible to the naked eye, the main star in the cluster, Mu Draconis A, is formally catalogued as Alrakis or *al-Raqis*, a traditional Arabic name meaning the trotting camel, or the dancer.[10] While in Frank Herbert's work the planet Arrakis only has a single sun, Mu Draconis is actually formed of three stars, which could serve to explain Dune's arid environment.

The Atreides homeworld of Caladan, meanwhile, is a relative solar neighbour, circling the bright star Delta Pavonis a mere 19.89 light years away from us. Visible in the southern hemisphere, the star can be seen in the constellation of Pavo, or the Peacock, and is one of the closest bright stars to Earth. At a similar distance of 19.5 light years away from Earth, though in another direction entirely, we find the constellation of Ophiuchus, an ancient Greek name meaning 'serpent bearer'. While the constellation contains several remarkable stars – including another of our closest neighbours, Barnard's Star, and RS Ophiuchi, which is thought to be on the brink of going supernova – Frank Herbert took inspiration from 36 Ophiuchi, another triple-star system made up of three orange dwarf stars caught in one another's gravity. It is around the second of these – 36 Ophiuchi B – that the Harkonnen home world of Giedi Prime revolves.

It is when dealing with the Spacing Guild, with its mutant navigators and heighliner spacecraft, that *Dune* feels most like a science-fiction novel. Elsewhere in the book, Frank Herbert takes pains to avoid the established trappings of the genre, replacing computers with mentats and holstering laser pistols in favour of swords and shields – he even wrote an entire chapter set on the Atreides frigate as it nestles in the belly of the vast Guild ship en route to Arrakis, then deleted it before publication.[11] But despite all this, *Dune* is still firmly a sci-fi novel, so let's explore some of the science-fiction stories that inspired its author, and fellow sci-fi writers who he was proud to call his friends.

In a 1973 interview, Frank Herbert claimed to have started reading the genre seriously 'in the early 40s. I'd been reading science fiction about 10 years before I decided to write it'.[12] But according to Brian his father's love of science fiction was there from boyhood: 'Every time Frank went fishing he tossed a book in his Boy Scout pack . . . H.G. Wells, Jules Verne and Edgar Rice Burroughs.'[13] Except for Verne, who died in 1905, these authors would still have been current when Herbert was coming of age, though Wells's great science-fiction works – *The Time Machine*, *The Island of Doctor Moreau*, *The Invisible Man*, *The War of the Worlds* and *The First Men in the Moon* – were already behind him (one final science-fiction masterpiece, *The Shape of Things to Come*, would arrive in 1933). We've already discussed the influence of Verne and Wells on *Dune*, so let's turn our attention to the third of those influences.

The tales of John Carter of Mars by *Tarzan* creator Edgar Rice Burroughs were one of the earliest examples of popular sci-fi, begun in 1911 and still widely read two decades later when Frank Herbert turned 11 years old. Following the adventures of an American Civil War soldier and 'Southern gentleman' who is mysteriously transported to the planet Mars – or Barsoom, in the local tongue – the stories were first serialized in *The All-Story* magazine as *Under the Moons of Mars*, and published as a single volume in 1917 with the title *A Princess of Mars*. Further instalments would follow at regular intervals, from 1918's *The Gods of Mars* to Rice Burroughs's final John Carter story, the gloriously titled 'Skeleton Men of Jupiter', in 1943. (In fact, spin-off titles are still being published, up to and including 2021's *John Carter of Mars: Gods of the Forgotten* by Geary Gravel.)

'The primary attraction of science fiction is that it helps us understand what it means to be human'

FRANK HERBERT, 'MEN ON OTHER PLANETS'[14]

Inspired by Percival Lowell and his vision of Mars as a once-thriving planet, Burroughs envisaged Barsoom as a desert world in steep decline, where wars over precious resources such as water and even air have become commonplace. Into this world steps John Carter, a courageous off-worlder who claims the hand in marriage of the Martian Princess, and ultimately rises to become the supreme Warlord of Mars. The inhabitants of Arrakis may not include four-armed egg-laying humanoids with tusks, but otherwise the parallels are striking. It's also worth noting again that Herbert considered setting his early version of *Dune* on Mars, before concluding that the planet was 'too familiar' to audiences – presumably, to those who had read Burroughs.

In that same *Vertex* interview, Herbert name-drops a few of his other sci-fi favourites including Robert A. Heinlein, whose stories – many of them published, like *Dune*, in *Analog* under the editorship of John Campbell – often focus on adolescent characters in a science-fiction setting. Heinlein's best-known novel, *Starship Troopers*, presents a world dominated by powerful elites, where human rights are strictly curtailed and prowess in battle is the highest form of honour. Herbert also mentions a pair of writers who were not just influences, but close personal friends: Jack Vance and Poul Anderson.

By the time of *Dune*'s publication, Vance, Herbert and their respective families had been close-knit for over a decade, travelling together to Mexico and sharing 'many fine dinners and outings',[15] particularly in the early 1960s when both families lived in the Bay Area. While his name may be less well known today, Vance had been a successful author long before Herbert, making his print debut with the short story 'The World-Thinker'[16] in 1945 while Frank Herbert was still taking writing classes at the University of Washington. Perhaps his best-known work would arrive in 1950: *The Dying Earth*, a collection of stories set in a far-flung future when the Sun is on the verge of collapsing and the people of the darkened Earth have rediscovered magic, becoming fanatically religious and decadent in the process. Republished in 1966 as a 'fix-up' novel compiled from these stories and leading to two sequels, the book's impact on Herbert is unmistakeable: a barren world, a degenerate population and widespread religious zealotry.

But Vance's influence on Herbert is also evident in less direct ways. In 1957, under the pseudonym Peter Held, Vance published his first mystery novel, *Take My Face* (its author preferred the marginally less lurid original title *The Flesh Mask*). Over the next three decades Vance would write many more thrillers, sometimes under the name Ellery Queen, but often as himself. For Herbert, this would have been proof that the term 'science-fiction writer' need not be a straitjacket: though sci-fi would remain his first love (and his most

TOP LEFT: Lifelong friends: Jack Vance (left) and the young Frank Herbert (right) in Kenwood, California, c. 1952

TOP RIGHT: A battle on Barsoom, from Edgar Rice Burroughs's *Thuvia, Maid of Mars*

BOTTOM: Caspar Van Dien combats the bug menace in the 1997 film of Robert A. Heinlein's *Starship Troopers*

'Do you want an absolute prediction? Then you want only today, and you reject tomorrow.'

FRANK HERBERT, 'DUNE GENESIS'

reliable meal ticket), he would also feel emboldened to write works of 'straight' fiction, notably *Soul Catcher*.

Vance would also beat Herbert to the Hugo Awards, taking the 1963 Best Short Story prize for his sci-fi/fantasy tale 'The Dragon Masters'. He'd win again in 1967, the year after *Dune*: this time the award was for Best Novelette, for Vance's ripely political tale of alien rebellion, 'The Last Castle'. He would continue to write long after his friend Frank Herbert's death, too, despite the fact that in the mid-1980s he was declared legally blind. He even managed to win one final Hugo Award in 2010, for his memoir *This is Me . . . Jack Vance*, published three years before his death.

Vance and Herbert didn't just share a love of writing, however; both men were also avid sailors. In 1962, along with another writer, Poul Anderson, they built a houseboat that they sailed up the Sacramento Delta from San Francisco Bay. The boat sank the same year, to the cash-strapped Herbert's chagrin, but the three men would remain fast friends, even intending to write an underwater adventure story together, though this plan never came to fruition.

Like Vance, Poul Anderson is another writer whose popularity has been eclipsed in recent years, though at his peak he was one of the most respected science-fiction authors in the world, winning no less than seven Hugo Awards for his short and mid-length fiction between 1961 and 1982. As with Vance and Herbert, Anderson did not restrict himself to the sci-fi genre. His best-known novel, 1954's *The Broken Sword*, was set in a fictionalized Viking era and fuses Norse mythology with high fantasy staples like elves and witches. His 1960 book *The High Crusade* may have been an influence on Herbert in the way it melded sci-fi with medieval adventure, as a shipload of invading aliens find their advanced technology no match for human hand-to-hand combat. But the vast majority of his work was in the short form: Anderson would publish hundreds of stories in his lifetime, becoming, in the words of the *Science Fiction Encyclopaedia*, 'perhaps science-fiction's most prolific writer of any consistent quality'.[17]

However, several Herbert scholars have argued that the single biggest science-fiction influence on *Dune* wasn't the work of a lifelong friend or a favourite from childhood. Rather, Herbert may have taken a kind of 'reverse inspiration' for *Dune* and its sequels from a series of books that he admired, but took great pleasure in picking apart: the *Foundation* trilogy by Isaac Asimov.

Published as a series of interlinked short stories between 1942 and 1950, they would be compiled into three hugely successful novels – *Foundation* (1951), *Foundation and Empire* (1952) and *Second Foundation* (1953). In 1966, the same year that Herbert shared Best Novel, Asimov would win a one-off Hugo Award for Best All-Time Series, and it's fair to say that, in the pre-*Dune* period, the *Foundation* books were the most highly regarded works of science fiction since Wells.

Like Herbert, Asimov took inspiration from historical texts, particularly those such as Edward Gibbon's *Decline and Fall of the Roman Empire*, which concern themselves with the ebb and flow of civilizations.[18] The resulting parallels are, again, self-evident: in a future so distant that Earth has become a myth, humanity is ruled by a vast, millennia-old galactic Empire whose elite rulers have become entirely remote from the people they're supposed to govern. Into this changeless universe steps a man with the professed gift of prophecy: the ability to predict the future, and thereby to influence it. His coming will alter the world forever.

In *Foundation,* the prophet in question is Hari Seldon, a mathematician who has formulated a new science that he names psychohistory: the ability to predict, within

LEFT: Linked 1973 covers for Isaac Asimov's *Foundation* trilogy

ABOVE: Frank Herbert's close friend, sci-fi master Poul Anderson

certain parameters of probability, the movements of large numbers of people, and thereby to make educated guesses about the future of humanity. But when he claims that the Empire's days are numbered, Seldon is arrested and exiled to the barren planet of Terminus, there to begin compiling a great store of knowledge – an *Encyclopaedia Galactica* – to help rescue humanity from the 'dark age' that he knows is coming.

For Seldon, science will light the way to a new future and be the saviour of a humanity lost to barbarism. His creator felt the same, and believed that science fiction ought to reflect this: he might not have named Herbert specifically, but it's hard not to think of *Dune* when Asimov writes: 'There is a growing tendency to delete the science from science fiction . . . There are science-fiction writers who think that science is a Bad Thing and that science fiction is a wonderful field in which to make this plain.'[19]

For Herbert, however, Asimov's ideas were much too simplistic. In his 1974 essay 'Science Fiction and a World in Crisis' he writes that, in a strictly controlled universe like the one in *Foundation*, 'the holders of power . . . have not awakened to the realization that there is no single model of a society, a species, or an individual'.[20] Two years later, in his essay 'Men on Other Planets', he'd go further, singling out *Foundation* and describing it as 'beautifully constructed' before taking its ideas to pieces in typically precise fashion. '*Foundation* history,' Herbert writes, '. . . is manipulated for larger ends and for the greater good as determined by a scientific aristocracy. It is assumed, then, that the scientist-shamans know best which course humanity should take.'[21]

For Herbert, the idea that the mass of people is somehow predictable, or that a cabal of scientists and psychologists could or should have the ability to control that mass, runs completely counter to his belief in the individual's capability, and indeed their right, to affect their world, intentionally or otherwise. As Tim O'Reilly writes, while the *Foundation* books prize rationality above all else, '*Dune* proclaims the power and primacy of the unconscious and the unexpected in human affairs'.[22]

Perhaps the closest parallel to Asimov's *Foundation* in Herbert's work are the Bene Gesserit, whose centuries-long efforts to steer the course of humanity and create their own 'super-being' are undermined at the final hurdle by the most human and emotional of choices, as Jessica makes the reproductive decision to give her Duke a son, rather than the daughter that the Bene Gesserit demanded. And when that super-being does arrive – unexpectedly, and in the wrong place – all he discovers is that people cannot be controlled, and that humanity's very randomness is one of the keys to what Herbert terms its 'vitality' as a species. Through the course of later books, as Herbert – like Asimov – peers further and further into his invented future, small, unpredictable acts, such as Jessica's, will have greater and greater consequences, and any further efforts to control the galactic population will be doomed to failure.

There's no question that Herbert admired Asimov and found his writing and his ideas tremendously stimulating; he was simply, as we've seen time and again, a sceptical and free-thinking person. As he wrote in 'Science Fiction and a World in Crisis': 'If you want a gold mine of science-fiction material, pull the assumptions out of the current best-seller list. Turn those assumptions over, look at them from every angle you can imagine. Tear them apart. Put them back together.'[23] Here, perhaps, is the Frank Herbert philosophy in a nutshell: question everything, examine everything – even, or perhaps especially, your own work. It was only by taking every orthodoxy apart, by seizing inspiration from a multiplicity of diverse, seemingly contradictory sources, that he was able to create a work of fiction as thematically rich, as intellectually self-examining and as eternally fascinating as *Dune*.

TOP: Jared Harris as 'psychohistorian' Hari Seldon in the 2021 TV adaptation of *Foundation*

BOTTOM LEFT: Frank Herbert's highly respected 'anti-influence': legendary sci-fi author Isaac Asimov

BOTTOM RIGHT: Manipulators of humanity: the Bene Gesserit as depicted in the 1984 film of *Dune*

EPILOGUE

DUNE WORLD

To create *Dune,* Frank Herbert drew on an endless variety of sources: historical, fictional, religious, scientific, highbrow, mass-market, obscure and obvious. But if anything, the cultural impact of his work has gone on to outstrip its inspirations: *Dune* is probably the most widely read sci-fi novel in history, and it is without doubt the most influential. As sci-fi scholar John J. Pierce attests: '*Dune* is to science fiction what *The Lord of the Rings* is to fantasy: the ultimate created world.'[1]

And while it may be largely coincidence that many of the themes in *Dune,* while relatively obscure when Frank Herbert was writing, would by the end of the 1960s have become commonplace, it might also be the case that *Dune*'s presence sped them along. As Tim O'Reilly writes: 'Oriental religion had not yet become widely popular in the West . . . Nonverbal communication was a little-known branch of ethnography. Altered states of consciousness were not considered a fit subject for research . . . It is a masterwork of imaginative science to proceed from such small beginnings to their flowering in *Dune.* The touchstone of their brilliance is not only that they have proved predictive, but that they seem obvious in retrospect.'[2]

Not that *Dune*'s influence was detectable right away. The book was far from being an immediate best seller, and it certainly wasn't followed by a flurry of sci-fi stories about troubled messiahs and desert worlds. Indeed, for its first decade, *Dune*'s popularity was largely confined to college students, and to science-fiction enthusiasts and fellow authors like Robert A. Heinlein and Arthur C. Clarke. Other notable early adopters included the crew of NASA's fifth moon mission, Apollo 15, who named a crater near their landing site 'Dune' after setting foot on its south ridge in 1971.[3]

That same year, the film rights to *Dune* were first optioned and offered to *Lawrence of Arabia* director David Lean, who perhaps unsurprisingly turned the project down (what his very British sensibilities would've made of the Fremen and their spice-fuelled orgies is anyone's guess). It wasn't until 1974, more than a decade after its first serialization, that a concerted attempt was made to mount a film version of *Dune* – though how practical those efforts were remains up for debate.

Under the guidance of the visionary Chilean film director, Tarot enthusiast and psychedelic explorer Alejandro Jodorowsky, this version of Herbert's book would have run some 14 hours in length, starred everyone from Orson Welles as Baron Harkonnen to Salvador Dalí as the Padishah Emperor, and cost considerably more money than any film up to that point, sci-fi or otherwise. The script took extreme liberties with Herbert's work: Duke Leto was depicted as a eunuch after being gored by a bull and Paul was the messianic child of a form of parthenogenesis using extracted blood. The design work produced by Jodorowsky and his collaborators, whose ranks included French comic book artist Jean Giraud a.k.a. Moebius, Austrian body-horror

icon H.R. Giger and British design genius Chris Foss, are simply mind-boggling, a total reimagining of Herbert's universe that is at once beautiful and totally berserk. By 1976 the project had collapsed, and it exists now only as enticing, hallucinatory fragments: dizzying scripts and storyboards, and a fascinating documentary entitled *Jodorowsky's Dune*.[4] Perhaps that's all it could ever have been.

The following year, however, a film would blast onto screens that incorporated many of *Dune*'s core elements, retooled for a mass audience. On the fringes of a multi-planetary Galactic Empire lies a remote desert world, home to a young moisture farmer with dreams of greatness. On a visit to the Dune Sea he has a run-in with a tribe of ferocious natives, and meets a hooded figure who imparts his knowledge of a unique form of mind-body discipline that will eventually allow the hero to defeat the mysterious emperor and restore balance to the galaxy.

Alerted by his son Brian, Frank Herbert would attend a screening of *Star Wars* in 1977, emerging with a list of 16 points of what he termed 'absolute identity' with *Dune*.[5] He wasn't alone: several other science-fiction writers also saw their work reflected in the year's biggest film, banding together to form what Herbert jokingly referred to as the We're Too Big To Sue George Lucas Society. Later films in the series must have riled Herbert even further, assuming he watched them: in *The Empire Strikes Back* we learn that Luke Skywalker is, like Paul Atreides, a direct descendant of the films' chief villain, while in *Return of the Jedi* we meet a vile, decadent, lizard-like creature called Jabba the Hutt who resembles nothing so much as Baron Harkonnen spliced with a sandworm.

What Herbert didn't know was that things could have been worse: in initial drafts, the quasi-religious order at the heart of *Star Wars* was referred to as the Jedi-Bendu, a clear nod to Herbert's discipline of *prana-bindu*, while some drafts featured a battle on the planet of Yavin where tribes of primitive Wookiees took up arms against the technologically advanced Empire – an idea revisited with the Ewok rebellion in *Return of the Jedi*. It wasn't until *Heretics of Dune* in 1984 that Herbert would take what appears to be a very subtle form of revenge, slipping in a brief passage – '"He's a three P-O," they said, meaning that such a person surrounded himself with cheap copies'[6] – that seems to offer a sly dig at the perceived falseness of *Star Wars* and its robot character C-3PO,

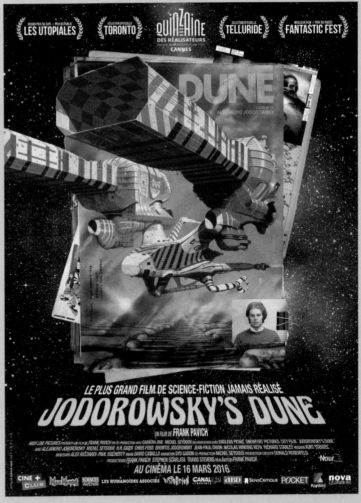

TOP LEFT: Apollo 15 astronauts David Scott, Alfred Worden and James Irwin

BOTTOM LEFT: Wild ambition: director Alejandro Jodorowsky (left), illustrator Jean 'Moebius' Giraud (right) and a costumed Sardaukar warrior

RIGHT: The poster for the 2013 documentary *Jodorowsky's Dune*

'I loved all the actors; I loved the crew; I loved working in Mexico; I loved everything except that I didn't have final cut'

DAVID LYNCH, ON *DUNE*[7]

known as Threepio. By then, of course, *Dune* would finally have its own big-screen adaptation – though the reception it received may not have been all that Frank Herbert hoped for.

Italian super-producer Dino De Laurentiis acquired the rights to *Dune* following the collapse of the Jodorowsky film in 1976, asking Frank Herbert himself to pen a screenplay. What became of that script is unknown, because almost immediately De Laurentiis changed tack, hiring offbeat American novelist Rudy Wurlitzer to reimagine the film, and bringing in Ridley Scott, fresh from *Alien*, to direct. Coincidentally, *Alien* had itself incorporated several unused elements from Jodorowsky's *Dune*, thanks to the presence of designer H.R. Giger and effects-supervisor-turned-writer Dan O'Bannon, whose idea *Alien* had been in the first place.

But again, failure beckoned: Scott pulled out following the death of his brother, and the Wurlitzer script was tossed onto the growing pile of *Dune* rejects. Instead, De Laurentiis turned to another bold young director: David Lynch, a renowned visual stylist in high demand following the success of *The Elephant Man*. Working with writers Christopher De Vore and Eric Bergren, Lynch initially split *Dune* into two scripts before the decision was made to attempt a one-film adaptation, cramming the entire plot into a single, epic motion picture. When De Vore and Bergren left, Lynch completed the work alone – his seventh draft would become the eventual shooting script.

The saga of David Lynch's *Dune* has been retold many times – the hefty budget, the troubled production in Mexico with its power cuts and communication blackouts, the employment of something like 20,000 extras. But it was when shooting ended that the real problems began, as Lynch turned in a three-hour movie only for Universal Pictures to demand that an hour be taken out. Dino De Laurentiis and his daughter Rafaella ended up shooting several 'bridging' scenes themselves in an effort to condense the plot, resulting in a 137-minute final cut.

And yet, on its release, Frank Herbert pronounced himself well pleased with the result. 'They've got it,' he told *People* magazine. 'There are some interpretations and liberties, but you're gonna come out knowing you've seen *Dune*.'[8] And looking back, it's perhaps easy to see

TOP: Swiss artist H.R. Giger's 1975 piece *Dune II* features an unused design for the Harkonnen castle on Giedi Prime

BOTTOM LEFT: The beast: there are clear echoes between Giger's designs for *Dune* and his later work on 1979's *Alien*

BOTTOM RIGHT: Ambitious young director David Lynch (right) on the set of 1980's *The Elephant Man*

'Give us a tune, Gurney'

DUKE LETO ATREIDES, *DUNE*[9]

why Herbert was pleased. The film captures the grand sweep of the novel, from the Shakespearian hallways of Caladan to the open deserts of Arrakis, from the fleshy, fishy Guild Navigator to the monstrous, only slightly plastic-looking *shai hulud*. The cast was filled with notable character actors: Patrick Stewart, Freddie Jones and Dean Stockwell make a winning triumvirate as Gurney Halleck, Thufir Hawat and Dr Yueh respectively, with memorably villainous turns from Jose Ferrer as the moustache-twirling Emperor and Brad Dourif as a marvellously vile Piter De Vries. But the acting honours were stolen by Kenneth McMillan as the monstrous Baron, a pustulent, floating flesh-balloon with a penchant for murdering innocent boys; he might be the most revolting villain ever put on screen, absolutely nailing the grotesquery of Herbert's creation.

If only audiences and critics had felt the same as the author. The reviews were dreadful: 'an incomprehensible, ugly, unstructured, pointless excursion into the murkier realms of one of the most confusing screenplays of all time,'[10] wrote America's leading critic Roger Ebert, effectively sealing the film's fate. The problem was that, while Lynch's script may have crammed as much as possible of Herbert's book into a single film, this left precious little time to explain anything to the viewer: audiences would sit baffled, unable to process the barrage of unfamiliar terms being thrown at them, or the cavalcade of bizarrely dressed characters marching across the screen. The violence, too, was extreme for a major blockbuster – McMillan's Baron may thrill *Dune* fans, but he must have seemed genuinely nightmarish to newcomers, especially kids expecting the latest *Star Wars* riff.

None of which prevented Universal from attempting to sell the film in the time-honoured, Lucas-inspired fashion: by producing toys, board games, colouring books and other memorabilia. The *Dune* action-figure line remains one of the oddest toy collections in movie history, with plastic figurines of the Baron, Feyd-Rautha, Rabban and the Sardaukar, each of them carrying miniature knives and pistols to fend off a tiny, flexible sandworm (of course, they now sell to collectors for absurd amounts of money). Meanwhile, the novel was condensed into *The Dune Storybook*[11] for younger readers – what the intended audience made of, say, the infant Alia slaughtering wounded warriors on the battlefield remains undocumented.

But the saga of David Lynch's *Dune* may not be over. In a 2021 interview, the director entertained for the first time the possibility of revisiting the excised footage. 'The thing was a horrible sadness and failure to me,' Lynch recalled. 'I sold out before I finished. But I would like to see what is there . . . there could be something.'[12] Whether this could ultimately lead to a new director's cut remains in doubt: 'I don't think it's a silk purse,' he admitted. 'I know it's a sow's ear.'[13] But the mere fact that he's willing to discuss the project after decades of silence is intriguing.

In the 1970s, music based on popular works of literature was all the rage, from Swedish progressive rocker Bo Hansson's *Music Inspired by Lord of the Rings* to David Bowie's *1984*-inspired suite on the album *Diamond Dogs*. *Dune* was no exception, kicking off with a hat-trick of synthesizer workouts created by three European electronic wizards.

In 1978, Frenchman Richard Pinhas created *Chronolyse*, a shimmering instrumental LP featuring

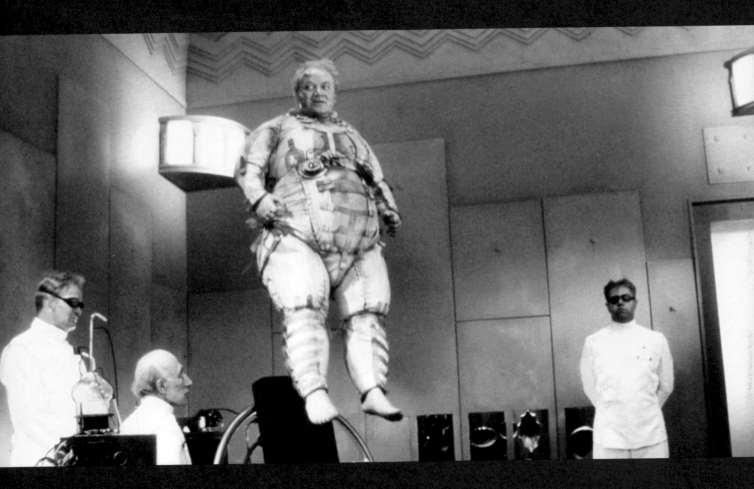

TOP: Hello, Arrakis! Iron
Maiden on stage in 1983

BOTTOM: *Geidi Primes*: the
2010 debut album by Grimes
was inspired by her love
of *Dune*

tracks entitled 'Paul Atreides', 'Duncan Idaho' and the seven-part 'Variations sur le thème des Bene Gesserit',[14] while the following year saw the release of German composer and former Tangerine Dream member Klaus Schulze's *Dune*,[15] with spoken-word contributions from flame-hatted 60s eccentric and self-proclaimed God of Hellfire, Arthur Brown. That same year, *Visions of Dune* by French musician Bernard Szajner, a.k.a. Zed,[16] would cap this unplanned trilogy, offering sumptuous, glittering drones and providing the ideal soundtrack to reading (and indeed writing) this book.

But it wasn't all ambient electronica. At the other end of the spectrum, British heavy-metal icons Iron Maiden penned a track entitled 'Dune' for their fourth LP, 1983's *Piece of Mind*, only to have their efforts derided by Frank Herbert's representatives. 'Frank Herbert doesn't like rock bands,' they wrote, in a tone uncannily redolent of the author himself, 'particularly heavy rock bands, and especially bands like Iron Maiden.'[17] It's easy to see why Herbert's people baulked: ultimately released under the title 'To Tame a Land', the song's lyrics range from the absurd – 'Without a stillsuit you would fry, on the sands so hot and dry, in a world called Arrakis!'[18] – to others suggesting that the band hadn't fully come to grips with the complex themes *Dune* was attempting to convey: 'Messiah supreme, true leader of men! And when the time for judgement's at hand, don't fret, he's strong, he'll make a stand against evil.'[19]

But *Dune*'s noisier fans would not be put off. In 1993, American metal band Fear Factory would release an industrial EP entitled *Fear is the Mind-Killer*,[20] while 1995 would see the formation in Florida of prog-hardcore band Shai Hulud. Again, the book's influence would prove global, from German death-metallers Golem, with their 1998 *Dune*-inspired concept album *The 2nd Moon*,[21] to British dance-pop artist Fatboy Slim, whose 2001 single 'Weapon of Choice' features the repeated lyric 'walk without rhythm, it won't attract the worm'.

But perhaps the most committed *Dune* tribute would come from a wholly unexpected source: pop icon and tabloid-bait in waiting, Grimes. In 2010, the artist born Claire Elise Boucher released her self-produced debut LP *Geidi Primes*, a dreamy and experimental concept album inspired by her favourite novel and featuring tracks entitled 'Caladan', 'Feyd Rautha Dark Heart' and 'Shadout Mapes'. She would later, of course, become romantically linked with the world's then-wealthiest

man – fellow *Dune* enthusiast, Elon Musk – before controversially abandoning him for anti-establishment whistle-blower, Chelsea Manning. What Frank Herbert would have made of all this can only be imagined.

The influence of *Dune* on literature has been rather subtler, even in the field of science fiction: while it's tempting to describe any science-fiction novel set on a barren world as post-*Dune*, that trope had, as we've seen, been around since Edgar Rice Burroughs. Our neighbouring planet was still inspiring new authors, however, and 1992 saw the release of *Red Mars* by Kim Stanley Robinson, the first in a trilogy of novels that would bring a new level of scientific rigour to science fiction.

Robinson was a confirmed *Dune* fan, having first encountered the book on a college road trip. 'I would read by flashlight,' he recalled later. 'I would read in tents, I would read in the back seat of the car when other people were driving. I was very impressed.'[22] Taking the familiar concept of human settlements on Mars and extrapolating it across years, decades and generations, Robinson's trilogy took a meticulous scientific approach to the kind of whole-planet climate transformation suggested in Herbert's books. So, while the *Mars* trilogy may be more pragmatic and less wildly imaginative than *Dune*, the influence of Herbert is present in its ecology, its wealth of detail and the scale of its imagined future.

In more recent years, *Dune* has been claimed as a key precursor to an ongoing wave of 'climate fiction' whose ranks include Robinson's *Science in the Capital* series, Cormac McCarthy's *The Road*, Margaret Atwood's *Oryx and Crake* novels and this author's own *FloodWorld* trilogy.[23] Inspired by the pressing climate threats that humanity is currently facing, these books echo Herbert in their concern with global ecology, and the ways human beings find to survive even in the most inhospitable environments.

It's in science-fiction cinema, however, that we find the clearest impression of Herbert's work. In 1984, long before films like *Princess Mononoke* and *Spirited Away* would rocket him to global stardom, filmmaker Hayao Miyazaki adapted his own manga comic *Nausicaa of the Valley of the Wind* into a soaringly imaginative animated film that would later be referred to as 'anime's answer to *Dune*'.[24] Set on Earth following a nuclear apocalypse, the film is an ecological parable set in an inhospitable wilderness – in this case, a globe-spanning jungle – teeming with giant creatures, whose people await the coming of a long-prophesied messiah.

A rather less serious but equally unmistakeable tribute to *Dune* may also be found in the lively 1990 horror comedy *Tremors*, in which the citizens of a remote Nevada town fall victim to an attack by monstrous, burrowing sandworms known as 'graboids'. With six low-budget sequels and a TV spinoff, the *Tremors* universe has become almost as expansive as Herbert's, if not quite as culturally significant.

It was in another area entirely, however, that *Dune* would leave perhaps its most indelible cultural mark. The first video game adaptation of Frank Herbert's novel would arrive in 1992: incorporating visual elements from the 1984 film, *Dune*'s moderate success would be overshadowed later the same year in the form of a semi-sequel variously titled *Dune II: The Building of a Dynasty* or *Dune II: Battle for Arrakis*. Actually developed at the same time as the first game, *Dune II* would lead gamemakers to coin the term 'real-time strategy' – a style whereby multiple players can operate simultaneously within a limited space, in this case the planet Arrakis, to gather resources and build bases from which to wage war on their opponents. A huge seller on release, *Dune II* would lead to the creation of even bigger real-time strategy games such as *Age of Empires* and *Warcraft*.

The enduring popularity of *Dune II* may also have been a factor in the commissioning of the next screen adaptation of Frank Herbert's book. Produced by the Sci-Fi Channel and first broadcast in 2000, the 265-minute, three-part miniseries *Frank Herbert's Dune* may have been a relatively faithful adaptation of the book, with an impressive budget for a TV production at the time. But the sets, costumes and effects still look unconvincing, even when compared to the David Lynch film made 16 years earlier, while the garish depiction of Baron Harkonnen as a leather-clad sexual predator is arguably even more offensive than the original text.

None of which stopped the series from being a success, however, placing it among the highest-rated ever broadcast by the channel, and leading to an imaginative but similarly cheap-looking sequel, *Frank Herbert's Children of Dune*, in 2003. Smartly weaving together plot strands from the novels *Dune Messiah* and *Children of Dune*, this Emmy-winning effort is notable for bringing some of Herbert's more outlandish ideas to a mass audience, such as the bonding of Paul's son Leto II with a larval sandtrout.

ABOVE: Another desert world: cover artwork by Don Dixon for *Red Mars* by Kim Stanley Robinson

RIGHT: 'Anime's answer to Dune': the 1984 film *Nausicaä of the Valley of the Wind*

'*Life is a game whose rules you learn if you leap into it and play it to the hilt*'

DARWI ODRADE,
CHAPTERHOUSE: DUNE[25]

TOP LEFT: Saskia Reeves as Jessica and Alec Newman as a rather grown-up Paul in the 2000 miniseries *Dune*

BOTTOM LEFT: Paul's offspring Ghanima (Jessica Brooks) and Leto II (James McAvoy) in 2003's *Children of Dune*

RIGHT: Director Denis Villeneuve with actor Javier Bardem on the set of 2021's *Dune*

Over the ensuing decade, cinematic adaptations of *Dune* would repeatedly be announced and cancelled, including a 2008 film to be directed by Peter Berg of *Friday Night Lights* and *Battleship* fame,[26] and another in 2010 by *Taken* director Pierre Morel[27] (for fans, the collapse of both projects would seem a lucky escape).

It wasn't until 2016 that reports first arrived that Canadian filmmaker Denis Villeneuve, best known for intelligent blockbusters like *Sicario* (2015) and *Arrival* (2016), was in talks to direct a promising new adaptation, with Oscar-winner Eric Roth of *Forrest Gump* (1994) and *A Star is Born* (2018) on script duties.[28] The following year, an announcement was made that readers had long been praying for: this *Dune* would arrive as two films,[29] splitting the book down the middle and giving the story the space that it needed.

The release and popular success of Villeneuve's *Dune: Part One* in 2021 rekindled the public's fascination with Frank Herbert's work, while the confirmation that a sequel would follow in 2023 only deepened it. Villeneuve's film may have stripped the story of *Dune* back to its basics, focusing on the story of Paul and Jessica and diminishing key characters like Gurney Halleck and Thufir Hawat, but that allowed for more and greater surprises when fans of the film discovered the broader scope of the novel and its sequels.

But perhaps the most important impact of Frank Herbert and *Dune* has been in the area of ecology. *Dune* was intended by its author to act as 'an environmental awareness handbook'[30] alerting readers to the fragility of their environment and encouraging them to take part in protecting and restoring it, just as Frank and Beverly Herbert attempted to do with their Ecological Demonstration Project. Favourably reviewed in the inaugural 1968 edition of the counter-cultural commune-builder's bible *Whole Earth Catalog*, *Dune* appeared alongside articles on everything from tipi design and wilderness survival to cybernetics and the I Ching, described as a 'clear portrayal of the fierce environment it takes to cohere a community . . . The metaphor is ecology. The theme revolution'.[31] Frank Herbert may have made for an unlikely revolutionary, but when it came to the environment it's an entirely appropriate term. 'People are more important than things,' he would write in *New World or No World*, a book of interviews released to mark the first Earth Day in 1970. 'Humans are not objects of consumption. We must develop an absolute priority of humans ahead of profit – any humans ahead of any profit. Then we will survive . . . Together.'[32]

In the twenty-first century, this question of survival has become ever more pressing and the lessons of *Dune* more pertinent than ever, inspiring scientists, academics and environmentalists around the world. In a 2010 lecture

Stunning cover artwork by
Bruce Pennington from a
1968 edition of Dune

'When we speak of defending the environment, we are speaking of defending our own lives'

FRANK HERBERT, NEW WORLD OR NO WORLD

entitled 'The Road to Arrakis: *Dune* and a Sustainable Future,'[33] Professor of Evolutionary Anthropology, Dr John Bock, asked what lessons we might learn from the way Frank Herbert depicted entire communities taking responsibility for their environment. Meanwhile, Economics Professor Dr Denise Stanley's 2015 lecture 'Natural Resource Extraction Curses: Observations from *Dune*'s Spice and Red Lobster's Shrimp,[34] asked how the lessons of spice mining in *Dune* – given the limited nature of the resource, and the harsh environment of its extraction – could offer lessons for modern shrimp farmers and their poorly paid labourers.

One of those turning *Dune*'s imagined technologies into real-life objects is Daniel Fernandez, a science professor at California State University who has set up a system of 'fogcatchers' to gather water from the air, much like Fremen dew traps. In a 2015 lecture on the project and his methods,[35] Fernandez explored the influence of *Dune*, quoting key aphorisms such as Pardot Kynes's lesson that 'you must cultivate ecological literacy among the people,'[36] and contrasting the patience of the Fremen, with their acceptance of the 'self-imposed delay between desire for a thing and the act of reaching out to grasp that thing',[37] against our own tendency to prioritize material wealth above ecological concerns: placing profit before humans, just as Herbert warned.

It's hard to imagine a better outcome for Frank Herbert than to see his work inspiring not just artists, writers and filmmakers but also ecologists and scientists, making a definable impact on the future of our species. As the author wrote, echoing the words of Paul Bigelow Sears: 'the highest function of ecology is the understanding of consequences'[38] – for the individual, for the community, for the planet. When he first sat down to work on *Dune*, poring through his reams of research, compiling his folders, seeking out new avenues of exploration, envisioning whole worlds and finally writing, writing, writing, Frank Herbert cannot have had the faintest inkling of the personal, cultural and global consequences that would follow.

Endnotes

Note: Page references for *Dune* are taken from: Herbert, Frank. *Dune*, Hodder, London, 2005.

Introduction

1 'Dune Genesis'.
2 B. Herbert, 167.
3 *Dune*, 330.
4 W.E. Copland, 'Burley and its Location', *The Arena*, Boston, October 1902. Reprinted in S. Willis, 'There are No Grog Shops, Low Dance Halls, or Gambling Dens in Utopia: But There Are Cigars!', *From Our Corner*, 4 October 2012. (blogs.sos. wa.gov/fromourcorner/index. php/2012/10/there-are-no-grog-shops-low-dance-halls-or-gambling-dens-in-utopia-but-there-are-cigars)
5 C. Henry, *Kitsap Sun*, Washington, 14 January 2012, quoted in the above.
6 B. Herbert, 113.
7 W.E. McNelly, 1969.
8 Ibid.
9 F. Herbert, Liner notes to the LP *Sandworms of Dune*, Caedmon Records TC 1565, New York, 1978.
10 W.E. McNelly, 1969.
11 *God Emperor of Dune*, 173.
12 This original conception was later expanded into a novella, *Spice Planet*, by Brian Herbert and Kevin J. Anderson, working from Frank Herbert's notes, and published in the 2005 ephemera collection *The Road to Dune*.
13 B. Herbert, 169.
14 Quoted in G. Gaylard, 'Postcolonial Science Fiction: The Desert Planet', in *Science Fiction, Imperialism and the Third World*, McFarland and Co., Jefferson, NC, 2010, 21–36.
15 F. Herbert, 'Dune World', *Analog*, December 1963–February 1964.
16 F. Herbert, 'Prophet of Dune', *Analog*, January–May 1965.
17 J.W. Campbell, 'Who Goes There?' *Astounding Science Fiction*, August 1938.
18 *The Road to Dune*, 210.
19 Foreword to the first edition of *Heretics of Dune*.
20 R. Zelazny, *This Immortal*, Ace Books, New York, 1966.
21 J.R.R. Tolkien, letter to John Bush, 12 March 1966. Quoted in J. Eisenberg, 'Tolkien v. Herbert', *Writing For Your Life*, 23 April 2020. (medium.com/writing-for-your-life/tolkien-v-herbert-50c1a31487de)
22 Immerwahr, 2020.
23 D.R. Murray, *Shoptalk: Learning to Write with Writers*, Boynton/Cook, Portsmouth, NH, 1990..
24 E. Weiner, *National Lampoon's Doon*, Pocket Books, New York, 1984.
25 *Chapterhouse: Dune*, 473.
26 *Chapterhouse: Dune*, 475.
27 *Dune*, 251.

Chapter One

1 *Dune*, 5.
2 Foreword to *Heretics of Dune*.
3 *Dune*, 13.
4 B. Herbert, 62.
5 H.D. Thoreau, *Walden*, Ticknor and Fields, Boston, 1854.
6 P.S.K. Young, 'Camping Was So Popular It Became Basic and Nearly Ruined the "Outdoors"', *Daily Beast,* 15 May 2021. (thedailybeast. com/camping-was-so-popular-it-became-basic-and-nearly-ruined-the-outdoors)
7 W.W. Chafe, *The Unfinished Journey: America Since World War II,* Oxford University Press, New York, 1986. Quoted in R.J. Ellis.
8 B. MacDonald, *The Egg and I*, J. B. Lippincott, Philadelphia, 1945.
9 H. and S. Nearing, *Living the Good Life: How to Live Sanely and Simply in a Troubled World*, Social Science Institute, US, 1954.
10 J. Kerouac, *The Dharma Bums*, Viking Press, New York, 1958.
11 The Wilderness Act, Public Law 88-577 (16 USC. 1131–1136), US, 1964. Cited on *Wilderness Connect* (wilderness.net/learn-about-wilderness/key-laws/wilderness-act/default.php)
12 *The Road to Dune*, 198. The collection reprints Frank Herbert's proposal for 'They Stopped the Moving Sands', along with his correspondence.
13 *The Road to Dune*, 200.
14 J.E. Lovelock, 'Gaia as Seen Through the Atmosphere', *Atmospheric Environment*, Elsevier, Amsterdam, Netherlands, 1972.
15 K.S. Guthke, *The Last Frontier: Imagining Other Worlds from the Copernican Revolution to Modern Fiction*, Cornell University Press, Ithaca, 1990.
16 H.G. Wells, *The War of the Worlds*, William Heinemann, London, 1898, 1.
17 P.B. Sears, *Deserts on the March*, University of Oklahoma Press, Norman, 1935.
18 *Dune*, 314.
19 Parallel quotes from Sears and *Dune* cited in T. O'Reilly.
20 *Dune*, 570.
21 R. Carson, *Silent Spring*, Houghton Mifflin, Boston, 1962.
22 H.P. Hynes, *The Recurring Silent Spring*, Pergamon Press, New York, 1989.
23 R.J. Ellis.
24 *Dune*, 565.
25 *Dune*, 336.
26 *The Road to Dune*, 199.
27 W.E. McNelly, 1969.
28 *Dune*, 282.
29 *Dune*, 285.
30 J. Frazer.,*The Golden Bough*, Macmillan and Co, London, 1890.
31 J. Elkington, 232.
32 W.E. McNelly, 1969.
33 F. Herbert, liner notes to the LP *Sandworms of Dune*, Caedmon Records TC 1565, New York, 1978.
34 *Dune*, 239.
35 J.G. Workman, *Heart of Dryness: How the Last Bushmen Can Help Us Endure the Coming Age of Permanent Drought*, Walker & Co., New York, 2009.
36 *Dune*, 224.
37 J.G. Workman, *Heart of Dryness: How The Last Bushmen Can Help Us Endure The Coming Age of Permanent Drought*.
38 R. Wynberg, D. Schroeder and R. Chennells, *Indigenous Peoples, Consent and Benefit Sharing: Lessons from the San-Hoodia Case*, Springer Science and Business Media, Berlin, 2009.
39 L. van der Post, *The Lost World of the Kalahari*, Penguin, London, 1958.
40 S. Ouzman, 'Silencing and Sharing Southern Africa Indigenous and Embedded Knowledge' in C. Smith and H.M. Wobst (eds) *Indigenous Archaeologies: Decolonizing Theory and Practice,* Routledge, Taylor & Francis Group, Abingdon, 2004.
41 *Dune*, 132.

Chapter Two

1 L. Blanch, *The Sabres of Paradise*, John Murray, London, 1960.
2 M. Gammer, 'Empire and Mountains: The Case of Russia and the Caucasus', *Social Evolution and History*, Uchitel Publishing House, Volgograd, Russia, September 2013.
3 L. Blanch, *The Sabres of Paradise*.
4 L. Blanch, *The Wilder Shores of Love*, Phoenix Press, London, 1954.
5 L. Blanch, *Farah, Shahbanou of Iran: Queen of Persia*, Harper Collins, London, 1978.
6 *Dune*, 102.
7 A. Khan, 'How "The Sabre of Paradise" (sic) Inspired *Dune*', *Medium*, July 2020. (arnoldkhan.medium.com/how-the-sabre-of-paradise-inspired-dune-f2b892c4869e)
8 L. Blanch, *The Sabres of Paradise*, referenced in W. Collins.
9 *Dune*, 437.
10 W. Collins.
11 L. Blanch, *The Sabres of Paradise*, quoted in C. Shepherd, 'Dagestan's Warrior Priest', East of Elbrus, 23 July, 2021. (eastofelbrus.com/articles/dagestans-warrior-priest)
12 K. Kennedy, 2016.
13 *Dune*, 404.

14 A. Karjoo-Ravary, 'Frank Herbert's *Dune* novels were heavily influenced by Middle Eastern, Islamic cultures, says scholar', *CBC Radio*, October 2021. (cbc.ca/radio/day6/introducing-the-metaverse-crisis-in-afghanistan-stuff-the-british-stole-islamic-influence-in-dune-and-more-1.6220405/frank-herbert-s-dune-novels-were-heavily-influenced-by-middle-eastern-islamic-cultures-says-scholar-1.6221670)

15 K. Kennedy, 2016.

16 A. Karjoo-Ravary, *CBC Radio*, October 2021.

17 H. Durrani, October 2021.

18 K. Baheyeldin.

19 F. Daftary, *The Isma'ilis: Their History and Doctrines*, Cambridge University Press, Cambridge, 1990.

20 B. Lewis, *The Assassins: A Radical Sect in Islam*, Weidenfeld and Nicolson, London, 1967.

21 R. Da Pisa and M. Polo, *The Travels of Marco Polo*, c. 1300.

22 F. Daftary, *Historical Dictionary of the Ismailis*, Scarecrow Press, Maryland, 2012.

23 E. Burman, *The Assassins – Holy Killers of Islam*, Crucible, London, 1987.

24 J. von Hammer-Purgstall, *Die Geschichte der Assassinen aus morgenländischen Quellen (The History of the Assassins)*, Smith, Elder and Co, London, 1835.

25 V. Bartol, *Alamut*, Scala House Press, London, 1938.

26 W.S. Burroughs, 'The Last Words of Hassan Sabbah', poem written in 1960, but first printed in *Nova Express*, Grove Press, New York, 1964.

27 B. Herbert, 31.

28 *Dune*, 355.

29 G. Pettit, *The Quileute of La Push, 1775–1945*, University of California Press, US, 1950.

30 D. Immerwahr, 2022.

31 Ibid.

32 Ibid.

Chapter Three

1 *Dune*, 430.

2 *Dune*, 81.

3 *Dune*, 415.

4 T. O'Reilly, 'Conversations in Port Townsend', in *The Maker of Dune*, 238.

5 B. Herbert, 85.

6 P. Stamets, *Mycelium Running: How Mushrooms Can Help Save the World*, Ten Speed Press, Berkeley, 2005.

7 *Dune*, 411.

8 *Dune*, 511.

9 G.R. Wasson, 'Seeking the Magic Mushroom', *Life*, New York, May 1957.

10 *Dune*, 21.

11 M. Polidoro, *Final Seance: The Strange Friendship Between Houdini and Conan Doyle*, Prometheus Books, Amherst, New York, 2001.

12 J.B. Rhine, *Extra-Sensory Perception*, Faber & Faber, London, 1935.

13 W.S. Cox, 'An Experiment on Extra-Sensory Perception', *Journal of Experimental Psychology*, American Psychological Association, Washington DC, August 1936.

14 W.E. McNelly, 1969.

15 Ibid.

16 Foreword to *Heretics of Dune*.

17 B. Herbert, 223.

18 *Dune*, 341.

19 Heisenberg would also lend his name to another Frank Herbert project, his next-but-one novel after *Dune*: *Heisenberg's Eyes*, later retitled *The Eyes of Heisenberg* (Berkeley Books, New York, 1966). This novel envisions a future Earth ruled by the tyrannical Optimen, whose efforts to hold humanity in complete stasis are undermined by Heisenberg-like genetic uncertainties. Similar ideas would also fuel Herbert's later *God Emperor of Dune*.

20 W. Heisenberg, *Physics and Philosophy: The Revolution in Modern Science*, Harper, New York, 1958.

21 A. Einstein, 1926 letter to Max Born, published in I. Born (translator), *The Born–Einstein Letters*, Walker and Company, New York, 1971.

Chapter Four

1 *Dune*, 123.

2 *Dune*, 82.

3 B. Herbert, 178.

4 B. Herbert, 179.

5 *Dune*, 72.

6 B. Conrad, 'Bullfighting', *Britannica*, May 1999. (britannica.com/sports/bullfighting/History)

7 B. Herbert, 36.

8 *Dune*, 30.

9 Shakespeare, *Romeo and Juliet*, 1594/2003, Prologue: line 5.

10 K. Brennan, 'Dune', *Star Wars Origins*. (moongadget.com/origins/dune.html)

11 *Dune*, 14.

12 F. Herbert, liner notes to the LP *Dune (The Banquet Scene)*, Caedmon Records TC 1555, New York, 1977.

13 D. Villeneuve (director), *Dune*, Legendary Pictures, 2021.

14 T.M. Moore, 'Sciences of *Dune*: Ethnography', *Los Angeles Review of Books*, March 2022. (lareviewofbooks.org/article/ethnography).

15 *Dune*, 478.

16 D. Immerwahr, 2022.

Chapter Five

1 *Dune*, 319.

2 J. Elkington, 230.

3 F. Herbert, liner notes to the LP *Dune (The Banquet Scene)*, Caedmon Records TC 1555, New York, 1977.

4 B. Herbert, 182.

5 D. Green, *Three Empires on the Nile: The Victorian Jihad, 1869–1899*, Free Press, New York, 2007, 87.

6 Ibid.

7 *Dune Messiah*, 96.

8 *Dune*, 131.

9 N. Ferguson, *Empire: How Britain Made the Modern World*, Penguin Books, London, 2003. 267–72.

10 A.E.W. Mason, *The Four Feathers*, Macmillan, London, 1902.

11 B. Herbert, 22.

12 R. Kipling, 'The White Man's Burden' (1899), compiled in *Rudyard Kipling's Verse*, Doubleday, New York, 1940.

13 H.R. Harris, 'Don Shirley's family dismayed by *Green Book* Oscar wins, calls portrait of pianist false', *USA Today*, February 2019. (eu.usatoday.com/story/life/movies/academy-awards/2019/02/25/don-shirleys-family-green-book/2979734002)

14 H. Durrani, 2020.

15 Ibid.

16 B. Herbert, 141.

17 J. Wilson, *Lawrence of Arabia: The Authorised Biography of T.E. Lawrence*, Atheneum, New York, 1990.

18 T.E. Lawrence, *Seven Pillars of Wisdom*, privately published, UK, 1926.

19 J. Wilson, *Lawrence of Arabia: The Authorised Biography of T.E. Lawrence*.

20 Interview with General Allenby, *The Listener*, May 1935. Transcribed by PBS. (pbs.org/lawrenceofarabia/players/allenby2.html)

21 D. Lean (director), *Lawrence of Arabia*, Columbia Pictures, 1962.

22 S. Lacy (director) *Spielberg*, HBO, 2017.

23 Interview with General Allenby, *The Listener*, May 1935.

24 *Dune*, 536.

25 W.E. McNelly, 1969.

26 T.E. Lawrence, *Seven Pillars of Wisdom*.

27 Ibid.

28 *Dune*, 572.

29 'Dune Genesis'.

30 W.E. McNelly, 1969.

Chapter Six

1 *The Road to Dune*, dedication (uncredited, but likely written by Brian Herbert).

2 J. Elkington.

3 F. Herbert, liner notes to the LP *Sandworms of Dune*, Caedmon Records TC 1565, New York, 1978.

4 Z. Sharf, 'Villeneuve Expands Lady Jessica Role in *Dune* to Make Her More Than "an Expensive Extra"', *IndieWire*, September 2020. (indiewire.com/2020/09/denis-villeneuve-expands-lady-jessica-role-dune-1234583740)

5   K. Kennedy (guest), '*Dune Scholar* interview', *Dune Pod* podcast, 18 April 2022. (solo.to/dunepod)
6   T. O'Reilly, 'Conversations in Port Townsend'.
7   Ibid.
8   *Chapterhouse: Dune,* 370.
9   K. Kennedy, 'Female Jesuits: The Catholic Origins of the Bene Gesserit', *Dune Scholar*, 19 Mar, 2020. (dunescholar.com/2021/03/19/female-jesuits-the-catholic-origins-of-the-bene-gesserit)
10 *Dune*, 597.
11 A. Korzybski, *Science and Sanity: An Introduction to Non-Aristotelian Systems and General Semantics*, International Non-Aristotelian Library Publishing Co, Lakeville, Connecticut, 1933.
12 R. Diekstra, *Haarlemmer Dagblad*, 1993, cited by L. Derks & J. Hollander, *Essenties van NLP*, Utrecht, Servire, 1996, 58.
13 S.I. Hayakawa, *Language in Thought and Action*, Harcourt, San Diego, 1949.
14 W.E. McNelly, 1969.
15 As Haris Durrani and others have pointed out, this oft-repeated quote from Dutch author and theosophist Jacobus Johannes van der Leeuw is often miscredited to Soren Kierkegaard. Either way, Frank Herbert left it uncredited when he borrowed it for *Dune*, 45.
16 *Dune*, 184.
17 A. Watts, *Behold the Spirit: A Study in the Necessity of Mystical Religion*, John Murray, London, 1947.
18 B. Herbert, 165.
19 Ibid.
20 M. Weingrad.
21 F. Galton, *Hereditary Genius*, Macmillan and Co, London, 1869.
22 I.W. Charny (ed), *Encyclopedia of Genocide*, *Volume 1*, ABC-CLIO, Santa Barbara, 2000.
23 T. Cohen, 'White Purity, Eugenics, and Mass Murder', Keene State College, May 2022. (keene.edu/academics/cchgs/resources/documents/white-purity-eugenics-and-mass-murder)
24 *Dune*, 58.
25 J.S. Carroll.

Chapter Seven
1   *Dune*, 296.
2   *Dune*, 371.
3   *Heretics of Dune*, 408.
4   *Dune*, 81.
5   Quoted in uncredited article 'Caligula', *History*, 16 December 2009. (history.com/topics/ancient-history/caligula)
6   *Dune*, 219.
7   *Dune*, 268.
8   B. Herbert, 250.
9   Ibid.
10 *God Emperor of Dune*, 342.
11 B. Herbert, 472.
12 B. Herbert, 180.
13 *Dune*, 98.
14 *Dune,* 273.
15 *Dune*, 429.
16 G.W. Trendle and F. Striker (created by), *The Green Hornet*, Twentieth Century Fox Television, 1966–67.
17 T. O'Reilly.

Chapter Eight
1   *Dune*, 594.
2   S. Butler, *Erewhon or, Over the Range*, Ballantyne, London, 1872.
3   S. Butler, 'Darwin among the Machines'.
4   S. Butler, *Erewhon or, Over the Range* (2nd ed), Grant Richard, London, 1901.
5   S. Butler, 'Darwin among the Machines', *The Press*, Christchurch, New Zealand, Jun 1863.
6   F. Herbert, '2068 AD', *San Francisco Sunday Examiner and Chronicle*, 28 July 1968.
7   *Without Me You're Nothing*.
8   T. O'Reilly, 'Conversations in Port Townsend', in *The Maker of Dune*, 233.
9   *Dune*, 23.
10 P. Stone.
11 B. Holland, 'Human Computers: The Women of NASA', *History*, December 2016. (history.com/news/human-computers-women-at-nasa)
12 *Dune*, 341.
13 B. Herbert, 34.
14 *Dune*, 413.
15 B. Herbert, 71.
16 C.G. Jung, 'The Structure of the Unconscious', *Collected Works of C.G. Jung, Volume 7*, Pantheon Books, New York, 1953.

17 C.G. Jung, 'The Structure and Dynamics of the Psyche' in *Collected Works of C.G. Jung, Volume 8,* Pantheon Books, New York, 1960.
18 C.G. Jung, 'Instinct and the Unconscious' in *Collected Works of C.G. Jung, Volume 8,* Pantheon Books, New York, 1960.
19 R.W. Semon, *The Mneme*, George Allen & Unwin, London, 1921.

Chapter Nine
1   *Dune*, 32.
2   *Dune,* 58.
3   Foreword to *Heretics of Dune*.
4   J.D. Colgan, *Partial Hegemony: Oil Politics and International Order*, Oxford University Press, Oxford, 2021.
5   *Dune,* 106.
6   'Science Fiction and a World in Crisis', in *The Maker of Dune,* 21.
7   K. Kennedy, 2021.
8   C. Anderson, N. Frykma, L.H. van Voss, Lex Heerma, M. Rediker (eds), *Mutiny and Maritime Radicalism in the Age of Revolution: A Global Survey*, Cambridge University Press, Cambridge, 2013.
9   V.C. Loth, 'Pioneers and Perkeniers: The Banda Islands in the Seventeenth Century', *Cakalele,* Volume 6, Honolulu, 1995, 13–35.

Chapter Ten
1   From *Dune: A Recorded Interview*, a cassette tape featuring interviews with Frank Herbert and David Lynch released ahead of Lynch's *Dune* movie. Waldentapes, US, 1983.
2   *Chapterhouse: Dune*, 59.
3   D. Immerwahr, 2020.
4   F. Herbert, 'Science Fiction and a World in Crisis', in *The Maker of Dune*, 41.
5   P. Stone.
6   *Dune*, 584.
7   *God Emperor of Dune*, 409.
8   *Dune*, 125.
9   *Dune: A Recorded Interview*, Waldentapes, US, 1983.
10 'Dune Genesis'.
11 *Dune*, 525.
12 *Dune*, 533.
13 R.D. McFadden, 'Reagan

Cites Islamic Scholar', *The New York Times*, New York, 2 October 1981, 26.
14 G. Thomas (writing as Quintus Curtius), 'The Rise and Fall of Empires: Ibn Khaldun's Theory of Social Development', *Quintus Curtius Fortress of the Mind*, May 2015. (hqcurtius.com/2015/05/08/the-rise-and-fall-of-empires-ibn-khalduns-theory-of-social-development)
15 'Ibn M_' (creator), *Ibn Khaldun and Dune: Introduction*, YouTube, Oct 2021. (youtube.com/watch?v=GHLndQ84ovg)
16 *Dune*, 296.
17 *Dune*, 434.
18 G. de la Bédoyère, 'The Praetorian Guard: the Emperors' Fatal Servants', *History Extra*, 16 Aug 2020. (historyextra.com/period/roman/the-emperors-fatal-servants)
19 Dattatreya Mandal, 'Janissaries: The Remarkable Origins and Military System of the Elite Soldiers', *Realm of History*, 19 Apr 2022. (realmofhistory.com/2022/04/19/facts-ottoman-janissaries)
20 P. Balfour and B. Kinross, *The Ottoman Centuries: The Rise and Fall of the Turkish Empire*, Perennial, London, 1977.
21 *Dune*, 600.

Chapter Eleven
1   *Dune*, 590.
2   *God Emperor of Dune*, 175.
3   M.M. Dunbar, 'Greenland During and Since the Second World War', *International Journal: Canada's Journal of Global Policy Analysis*, Volume 5, Issue 2, Canada, Jun 1950.
4   P.S. Mackenzie, Recorded interview with Frank Herbert No. 2, conducted 16 Jan 1977. Full transcript here: gwern.net/docs/fiction/science-fiction/frank-herbert/1977-mackenzie-frankherbertinterview.txt.
5   *Dune*, 593.
6   F.L. Ganshof, *Qu'est-ce que la féodalité (Feudalism)*, Longmans, London, 1952.

7   J.G. Griffiths, *The Divine Verdict: A Study of Divine Judgement in the Ancient Religions*, Brill, Leiden, Netherlands, 1991.

8   F. Gregorovius, *Wanderings in Corsica: Its History and Its Heroes*, Constable & Co, London, 1855.

9   K. Best, 'Hatfield-McCoy Feud Carries Lessons for Today', *University of Connecticut*, 10 September 2019. (today.uconn.edu/2019/09/hatfield-mccoy-feud-carries-lessons-today)

10 J. White, 'Peacemaker breaks the ancient grip of Albania's blood feuds', *The Christian Science Monitor*, 25 May 2008. (csmonitor.com/World/Europe/2008/0625/p01s02-woeu.html)

Chapter Twelve

1   *Children of Dune*, 147.
2   *Dune Messiah*, 11.
3   D. Knoop, *The Genesis of Freemasonry*, Manchester University Press, Manchester, 1947.
4   A. Conan Doyle, *The Sign of the Four*, Spencer Blackett, London, 1890.
5   D. Brown, *The Lost Symbol*, Doubleday, New York, 2009.
6   *Chapterhouse: Dune*, 14.
7   *God Emperor of Dune*, 250.
8   E.R. Burroughs, *A Princess of Mars*, AC McClurg, Chicago, 1917.
9   M.J. Daniels, 'The Stars and Planets of Frank Herbert's *Dune*: A Gazetteer', 1999. This painstakingly researched astronomical essay was published online in 1999, but the original link to it has expired. Thankfully, it has been widely reprinted and is easily searchable online.
10 P. Kunitzsch and T. Smart, *A Dictionary of Modern Star Names*, Sky & Telescope, Cambridge, Massachusetts, 2006.
11 This fascinating 'deleted scene' – along with several others – can be found in *The Road to Dune*, 248.
12 P. Turner, 34.
13 B. Herbert, 24.
14 'Men on Other Planets', in *The Maker of Dune*, 77.

15 B. Herbert, 161.
16 J. Vance, 'The World-Thinker', compiled in *The World-Thinker and Other Stories*, Spatterlight Press, Walnut, CA, 2017.
17 J. Clute and P. Nicholls, 31.
18 I. Asimov, *The Early Asimov*, Doubleday, New York, 1972.
19 Quoted in J.L. Grigsby, 150.
20 'Science Fiction and a World in Crisis' in *The Maker of Dune*, 45.
21 'Men on Other Planets', in *The Maker of Dune*, 80.
22 T. O'Reilly.
23 'Men on Other Planets', in *The Maker of Dune*, 83.

Epilogue

1   J.J. Pierce, *Foundations of Science Fiction: A Study in Imagination and Evolution*, Greenwood Press, Westport, Connecticut, 1987.
2   T. O'Reilly.
3   B. Herbert, 244.
4   F. Pavich (director), *Jodorowsky's Dune*, Sony Pictures Classics, 2013.
5   B. Herbert, 289.
6   *Heretics of Dune*, 350.
7   B. Simon, 'David Lynch on remastering Inland Empire, revisiting his earlier work and the chances of a *Dune* do-over', *The AV Club*, 14 April 2021. (avclub.com/david-lynch-inland-empire-interview-dune-restoration-1848795394)
8   L. Rozen, 'With Another Best-Seller and an Upcoming Film, *Dune* is Busting Out All Over For Frank Herbert', *People*, New York, 25 June 1984.
9   *Dune*, 159.
10 R. Ebert, *Dune* Review, *Chicago Sun Times*, Chicago, December 1984.
11 J.D. Vinge, *The Dune Storybook*, G.P. Putnam's Sons, New York, 1984.
12 B. Simon, 'David Lynch on remastering Inland Empire, revisiting his earlier work and the chances of a *Dune* do-over'.
13 Ibid.
14 R. Pinhas, *Chronolyse*, Cobra COB 37015, Paris, 1978.
15 K. Schulze, *Dune*, Brain 660.050, Hamburg, 1979.
16 Zed, *Visions of Dune*, Sonopresse 2S 068 16666, Paris, 1979.

17 M. Wall, *Iron Maiden: Run to the Hills, the Authorised Biography* (3rd ed.), Sanctuary Publishing, UK, 2004.
18 S.P. Harris (songwriter); Iron Maiden (performers), 'To Tame a Land', on *Piece of Mind*, EMI 1A 064-07724, Uden, Netherlands, 1983.
19 Ibid.
20 Fear Factory, *Fear is the Mindkiller*, Roadrunner RR 9082-2, New York, 1993.
21 Golem, *The Second Moon*, Ars Metalli ARS CD 008, Frankfurt, 1999.
22 A. Minoff, 'Meet the *Dune* Readers: Kim Stanley Robinson and Sara Imari Walker', *Science Friday*, 5 August 2014. (sciencefriday.com/articles/meet-the-dune-readers-kim-stanley-robinson-and-sara-imari-walker)
23 T. Huddleston, *FloodWorld* trilogy, starting with *FloodWorld*, Nosy Crow Books, London, 2019.
24 G. Yalcinkaya. 'How *Dune* inspired Hayao Miyazaki's *Nausicaä of the Valley of the Wind*, *Dazed*, 17 Sept, 2021. (dazeddigital.com/film-tv/article/54206/1/how-dune-inspired-hayao-miyazaki-s-nausicaa-of-the-valley-of-the-wind)
25 *Chapterhouse: Dune*, 45.
26 T. Siegel, 'Berg to direct *Dune* for Paramount', *Variety*, Los Angeles, 17 March 2008. (variety.com/2008/film/features/berg-to-direct-dune-for-paramount-1117982560)
27 N. Sperling, '*Dune* remake back on track with director Pierre Morel', *Entertainment Weekly*, New York, 4 January 2010.
28 J. Kroll, '*Forrest Gump* Writer Eric Roth to Pen Denis Villeneuve's *Dune* Reboot', *Variety*, Los Angeles, 5 April 2017. (variety.com/2017/film/news/dune-reboot-writer-eric-roth-denis-villeneuve-1201998001)
29 W. Hughes, 'Denis Villeneuve says he's now making two *Dune* movies, actually', *The AV Club*, Chicago, 9 Mar 2018. (avclub.com/denis-villeneuve-says-hes-now-making-two-dune-movies-1823660070)

30 *New World or No World*.
31 S. Brand (ed), *Whole Earth Catalog*, No 1010, Stewart Brand, Menlo Park, California, 1968, 43.
32 *New World or No World*.
33 J. Bock, 'The Road to Arrakis: *Dune* and a Sustainable Future', Pollak Library, California State University, 20 October 2015. (libraryguides.fullerton.edu/ld.php?content_id=17320963).
34 D. Stanley, 'Natural Resource Extraction Curses: Observations from *Dune*'s Spice and Red Lobster's Shrimp', Pollak Library, California State University, 23 October 2015.
35 D. Fernandez, 'Every Last Drop – Extracting Water from Fog', Pollak Library, California State University, 10 October 2015.
36 *Dune*, 315.
37 *Dune*, 333.
38 *Dune*, 314.

Two more eye-catching cover
designs by Bruce Pennington:
A 1972 edition of *Dune
Messiah* (top) and a 1977
paperback of *Children of
Dune* (bottom).

Bibliography

Works by Frank Herbert

The *Dune* series

- *Dune*, Chilton Books, Boston, Massachusetts, 1965.
- *Dune Messiah*, G.P. Putnam's Sons, New York, 1969.
- *Children of Dune*, G.P. Putnam's Sons, New York, 1976.
- *God Emperor of Dune*, G.P. Putnam's Sons, New York, 1981.
- *Heretics of Dune*, G.P. Putnam's Sons, New York, 1984.
- *Chapterhouse: Dune*, G.P. Putnam's Sons, New York, 1985.

Other works

- *The Dragon in the Sea* (a.k.a. *Under Pressure*), Doubleday & Co, New York, 1956.
- *The Green Brain* (a.k.a. *Greenslaves*), Ace Books, New York, 1966.
- *The Eyes of Heisenberg* (a.k.a. *Heisenberg's Eyes*), Berkley Books, New York, 1966.
- *The Santaroga Barrier*, Berkley Books, New York, 1968.
- *New World or No World* (editor), Ace Books, New York, 1970.
- *Soul Catcher*, G.P. Putnam's Sons, New York, 1972.
- *The Godmakers*, G.P. Putnam's Sons, New York, 1972.
- *Hellstrom's Hive*, Doubleday & Co, New York, 1973.
- 'Dune Genesis', *OMNI*, New York, Volume 2, No 10, July 1980, 72–75.
- *Without Me You're Nothing* (with Max Barnard), Simon & Schuster, New York, 1981.
- *Eye*, Berkley Books, New York, 1985.
- *The Maker of Dune: Insights of a Master of Science Fiction* (Tim O'Reilly, editor), Berkley Books, New York, 1987.
- *The Road to Dune* (with Brian Herbert and Kevin J. Anderson), Tor Books, New York, 2005.

Note: The above is only a partial Frank Herbert bibliography, citing works consulted for this volume.

Works by others

- Baheyeldin, Khalid. 'Arabic and Islamic themes in Frank Herbert's *Dune*', *The Baheyeldin Dynasty*, 22 January 2004. (baheyeldin.com/literature/arabic-and-islamic-themes-in-frank-herberts-dune.html)
- Carroll, Jordan S. 'Race Consciousness: Fascism and Frank Herbert's *Dune*', *Los Angeles Review of Books*, 19 November 2020. (lareviewofbooks.org/article/race-consciousness-fascism-and-frank-herberts-dune)
- Clute, John and Nicholls, Peter. *The Encyclopaedia of Science Fiction*, Orbit, London, 1993.
- Collins, Will. 'The Secret History of *Dune*', *Los Angeles Review of Books*, 16 September 2017. (lareviewofbooks.org/article/the-secret-history-of-dune)
- Durrani, Haris. '*Dune*'s Not a White Savior Narrative. But It's Complicated', *Medium*, 11 September 2020. (hdernity.medium.com/dunes-not-a-white-savior-narrative-but-it-s-complicated-53fbbec1b1dc)
- Durrani, Haris. 'The Muslimness of *Dune*: A Close Reading of "Appendix II: The Religion of *Dune*"', *Tor*, 18 October 2021. (tor.com/2021/10/18/the-muslimness-of-dune-a-close-reading-of-appendix-ii-the-religion-of-dune)
- Durrani, Haris. 'Sietchposting: A Short Guide to Recent Work on *Dune*', *Los Angeles Review of Books*, 27 March 2021. (lareviewofbooks.org/article/sietchposting-a-short-guide-to-recent-work-on-dune)
- Durrani, Haris and Cowles, Henry M. (eds). 'The Sciences of *Dune*', *Los Angeles Review of Books*, 27 March 2021. (lareviewofbooks.org/feature/sciences-of-dune-an-introduction)
- Elkington, John. 'Profile of Frank Herbert', *The Environmentalist*, Volume 1, Issue 3, Elsevier, Netherlands, Autumn 1981, 239–234.
- Ellis, R.J. 'Frank Herbert's *Dune* and the Discourse of Apocalyptic Ecologism' in R.J. Ellis & R. Garnett (eds). *Science Fiction Roots and Branches: Contemporary Critical Approaches*, Macmillan, London, 1990, 104–24.
- Grigsby, John L. 'Asimov's *Foundation* Trilogy and Herbert's *Dune* Trilogy: A Vision Reversed', *Science Fiction Studies*, Volume 8, No 2, SF-TH Inc, DePauw University, Indiana, July 1981, 149–55.
- Herbert, Brian. *Dreamer of Dune*, Tor Books, New York, 2003.
- Kennedy, Kara. 'Epic World-Building: Names and Cultures in *Dune*', *Names: A Journal of Onomastics*, Volume 64, Issue 2, Pitt Open Library Publishing, Pittsburgh, 2016, 99–108.
- Kennedy, Kara. 'Spice and Ecology in Herbert's *Dune*: Altering the Mind and the Planet', *Science Fiction Studies*, Volume 48, No 3, SF-TH Inc, DePauw University, Indiana, November 2021, 444–61.
- Immerwahr, Daniel. 'Heresies of *Dune*', *Los Angeles Review of Books*, 19 November 2020. (lareviewofbooks.org/article/heresies-of-dune)
- Immerwahr, Daniel. 'The Quileute *Dune*', *Journal of American Studies*, Volume 56, Issue 2, May 2022.
- Karjoo-Ravary, Ali. 'In *Dune*, Paul Atreides Led a Jihad, Not a Crusade', *Al Jazeera*, 11 October 2020. (aljazeera.com/opinions/2020/10/11/paul-atreides-led-a-jihad-not-a-crusade-heres-why-that-matters)
- McNelly, Willis E. *The Dune Encyclopaedia*, Berkley Books, New York, 1984.
- McNelly, Willis E. *Recording at the house of Frank Herbert*, 3 February 1969, original cassette digitized by California State University, Fullerton, available online at: archive.org/details/cfls_000091.
- O'Reilly, Tim. *Frank Herbert*, Frederick Ungar Publishing Co, New York, 1981.
- Ryding, Karin Christina. 'The Arabic of *Dune*', in D.F. Virdis, E. Zurru and E. Lahey (eds), *Language in Place: Stylistic Perspectives on Landscape, Place and Environment*, John Benjamins, Amsterdam, Netherlands, 2021.
- Stone, Pat. 'The Plowboy Interview: Frank Herbert, Science Fiction Author', *Mother Earth News*, Torpeka, Kansas, May 1981.
- Touponce, William F. *Frank Herbert*, Twayne Publishing, Boston, 1988.
- Turner, Paul. 'Vertex Interviews Frank Herbert', *Vertex: The Magazine of Science Fiction*, Volume 1, No 4, Los Angeles, October 1973, 34–37.
- Weingrad, Michael. 'Jews of *Dune*', Jewish Review of Books, Cleveland Heights, Ohio, 29 March 2015. (jewishreviewofbooks.com/articles/1633/jews-of-dune)

Index

Page numbers in *italics*
indicate illustration captions.

36 Ophiuchi 169

A

Agamemnon 66
Al Jazeera 98
Alien 181, 181
All-Story Magazine, The 169
Allenby, Edmund 85, 86
Amazing Stories 27
American Association
  of Science 27
American Society
  of Naturalists 27
Analog 14, 170
Anderson, Kevin J. 7, 18
  Hunters of Dune 18
  Sandworms of Dune 18
Anderson, Poul 170, *173*
  The Broken Sword 173
  The High Crusade 173
Annis, Francesca *94*
Apollo missions 125
  Apollo 15 *177*, 178, *179*
Arab Revolt 85–90, 135
Arabic culture 43–47, 75, 147
Aristotle 126
Arrival (2016) 189
artificial intelligence 122
Asimov, Isaac 7, *174*
  Foundation 173, 173–174,
  174
Assassins, Order of 44–47
Astounding Science Fiction 10
astronomy 164–169
Atwood, Margaret *Oryx
  and Crake* 185
Augustus 148

B

Baheyeldin, Khalid 44
Bang, Jette *156*
Bardem, Javier *188*
Barnard, Max *Without Me You're
  Nothing: The Essential Guide
  to Home Computers* 122–125
Barnard's Star 169
Bartol, Vladimir *Alamut* 47
Battleship 189
Beatles 101
Beau Geste 91
Bedouin 44, *44*, 85
Bell, Gertrude 86
Belmonte, Juan *65*, 71
Beowulf 33, 33, 91
Berg, Peter 189
Bergren, Eric 181
Biard, Pierre II *The Sacrifice
  of Iphigenia 66*
Black Death 147, 159

Blanch, Lesley *40*, 40
  Farah, Shahbanou of Iran 40
  The Sabres of Paradise
  40–43, 155
  The Wilder Shores of Love 40
Blassongame, Lurton 27, 30
blood feuds 160
Bock, John 192
Bolt, Robert 86
Boone and Crockett Club 24, *25*
Boone, Daniel *25*
Bosse, Abraham *159*
Boucher, Claire Elise *see* Grimes
Boule, Pierre *Planet of
  the Apes* 129
Bowie, David *Diamond Dogs* 182
Bradbury, Ray 27
Brooks, Jessica *188*
Brown, Arthur 185
Brown, Dan *The Lost Symbol* 164
bullfighting *65*, *71*, 71
Burley, Washington State 8
Burroughs, Edgar Rice 7, 8, 27,
  169–170, 185
  Gods of Mars 170
  Princess of Mars, A 169, 169
  'Skeleton Men of Jupiter' 170
  Thuvia, Maid of Mars 169,
  169, *170*
Burroughs, William S. 'The Last
  Words of Hassan Sabbah' 47
Butler, Samuel *Erewhon 122*, 122

C

Caligula *111*, 112, *149*, 149
Caligula (1979) 112
Calydon 66
Campbell, John W. 170
  'Who Goes There?' 14
Campbell, Joseph M. 61
Carson, Rachel *29*
  Silent Spring 29–30
Cartwright, Barbara 125
Catholicism 7, 94–97
Chalamet, Timothée *11*, *60*
Charlemagne 71
Charles, Prince 37
Charly (1968) 126
Chilton Books 14
Churchill, Winston 81, 85
Clarke, Arthur C. 14, 178
  Childhood's End 129, 129
Claudius 149
Cold War 115, *115*
collective unconscious 127
Collins, Will 'The Secret History
  of Dune' 43
colonialism 75, 81–82, 135
computers *121*, *125*, 125–126
Conrad of Montferrat 47
conservation 24
*Constitutions of the Free-Masons,
  The* 164
Cordon, Guy 10

counter-culture 57
Crandon, Mina 58

D

Dalí, Salvador 178
Dances with Wolves 82, 82
Daniels, Joseph M. 'The Stars and
  Planets of Frank Herbert's
  Dune: A Gazetteer' 169
Darwin, Charles 102
  On the Origin of Species 122
DDT 29–30
De Laurentiis, Dino 181
De Laurentiis, Rafaello 181
De Vore, Christopher 181
Defoe, Daniel *Robinson
  Crusoe* 81
Delta Pavonis 169
desert ecology 10–11, 23
  'desert creep' 24–27
  desertification 27–30
  human survival 33–37
Didius Julianus 149
Dirac, Paul 61
Doré, Gustave *46*
Douglas Fir Plywood
  Association 10
Dourif, Brad 182
Doyle, Arthur Conan 58, 99
  The Sign of Four 164
Dr Strangelove 115
Draco 169
Dune (1984) 17, 18, *86*, *94*, *112*,
  116, *125*, *144*, *165*, *174*,
  181–182, 186
Dune (2021) 11, 18, *33*, *36*, *54*,
  57, *60*, 75, *75*, 94, *94*, *97*, *116*,
  149, *188*, 189
Dune II 186
Durrani, Haris 44, 82
Dust Bowl *23*, 27, *29*
Dutch East India Company *135*,
  135–138, *138*

E

Ebert, Roger 182
Ecological Society of America 27
ecology 7, 8, 18, 48–51, 144,
  189–192
  Ecological Demonstration
  Project 16, 189
Edward I *46*
Einstein, Albert 61
El Cid 71
Elephant Man, The 181
Empire Strikes Back, The 178
Encyclopaedia of Genocide 102
Environmental Protection
  Agency 30
environmentalism 30, 48–51,
  189–192
Environmentalist, The 78
ESP (extra-sensory perception) 57
eugenics 102–104

F

Faisal, Prince 82, 86, *86*, 90
Fatboy Slim 'Weapon of Choice'
  185
Fear Factory 185
Ferguson, Rebecca *11*, 94, *94*,
  101
Fernandez, Daniel 192
Ferrer, Jose *144*, 182
feudalism 155–160
feuds 160
*Fierce Bull That Was Tamed,
  The* 71
First Nations people 51, *54*, 57
First World War 82–85
Ford, Gerald 164
Ford, John 51
Forrest Gump (1994) 189
Foss, Chris *167*, 178
Foundation (2021) 174
Fourth Anglo-Dutch War 138
Frank Herbert's Children of Dune
  186, *188*
Frank Herbert's Dune 186, *188*
Frazer, Sir James *The Golden
  Bough* 33
Freemasonry *163*, 164
Freud, Sigmund 127, *129*
Friday Night Lights 189
Fuseli, Henry *Macbeth, Banquo
  and the Witches 72*

G

Gaia hypothesis 27
Galton, Francis *104*
  Hereditary Genius 102
Gary, Romain 40
Gattaca 104, 104
gender roles 94
general semantics 98–99
Genghis Khan 91
Ghostbusters 58
Gibbon, Edward *Decline and Fall
  of the Roman Empire* 173
Giger, H.R. 178, *181*, 181
Gimry, Battle of *43*, 43
Giraud, Jean 178, *179*
Godfather Part II 160, *160*
Golem *The 2nd Moon* 185
Gomorrah 160, 160
Gordon, Charles 78, *78*
government *see* rulers
Gravel, Geary *John Carter of Mars:
  Gods of the Forgotten* 170
Great Depression 24, 27
Greece, ancient 66, 112, 160
Green Book 82
Green Hornet, The 116, 116
Greenland 156, *156*
Grimes *Geidi Primes 184*, 185
Gulf Wars 132–135, 147

Picture Credits

The publishers would like to thank the institutions, picture libraries, artists, galleries and photographers for their kind permission to reproduce the works featured in this book. Every effort has been made to trace all copyright holders but if any have been inadvertently overlooked, the publishers would be pleased to make the necessary arrangements at the first opportunity.

About The Author

Tom Huddleston is a freelance film and TV writer whose work has appeared in *The Guardian*, *Time Out* and *Little White Lies*, among others. He is the author of several sci-fi and fantasy novels for younger readers, including the acclaimed *FloodWorld* trilogy. He currently lives in London.

Acknowledgments

This book was enormous fun to write, and it's not often an author gets to say that. Thanks to John Parton at Quarto, who took a chance on someone who'd never written longform non-fiction before, and who was unstintingly enthusiastic and encouraging throughout. Thanks to Laura Bulbeck for her patient guidance through the citation minefield, and to Victoria Lympus for some pin-sharp copy-editing. Praise and gratitude to the *Dune* Scholar herself, Kara Kennedy, for her expert advice and precise critical eye – those notes were invaluable.

Like any good Bene Gesserit, my agent Ella Diamond Khan worked tirelessly behind the scenes to manipulate the situation for mutual benefit, while the unflinching support of my unbound concubine Rosie Greatorex kept the whole crusade rolling even when the moods and machinations of our very own genetic superman threatened to drive me screaming into the desert.

This is not a work of scholarly research; however, I drew upon the insight of countless experts and academics during the writing process. Daniel Immerwahr provided an invaluable list of resources and research avenues to follow, while Haris Durrani offered much-needed encouragement right at the start. Their writing on *Dune* – along with that of Kara Kennedy, Timothy O'Reilly, Karin Christina Ryding and many other very smart people – made this book possible.

Deirdre Noonan is the biggest *Dune*-head I know (and one of the very best people), so it'd be remiss of me not to give her a mention. I'll meet you down on the Southbank when it's time for Part 2 – I know you won't be late. Finally, David Jenkins was the catalyst for this entire business, so thanks again, old buddy. At the very least, I owe you a pint and a pie.